THE PSYCHOLOGY OF INVESTING

Fifth Edition

THE PSYCHOLOGY OF INVESTING

John R. Nofsinger
Washington State University

Routledge
Taylor & Francis Group

LONDON AND NEW YORK

First published 2014 2011, 2008, 2005, 2002 by Pearson Education, Inc.

Published 2016 by Routledge
2 Park Square, Milton Park, Abingdon, Oxon OX14 4RN
711 Third Avenue, New York, NY 10017, USA

Routledge is an imprint of the Taylor & Francis Group, an informa business

Credits and acknowledgments borrowed from other sources and reproduced, with permission, in this textbook appear on page 145.

ISBN: 9780132994897 (pbk)

Cover Designer: Suzanne Duda

Library of Congress Cataloging-in-Publication Data

Nofsinger, John R.
  The psychology of investing / John R. Nofsinger.—5th ed.
    p. cm.
  Includes index.
  ISBN-13: 978-0-13-299489-7

1. Investments—Psychological aspects.   I. Title.
  HG4515.15.N643 2014
  332.601'9—dc23

                                                                                    2012036304

10 9 8 7 6 5 4 3 2 1

CONTENTS

PREFACE

An old Wall Street adage states that two factors move the market: fear and greed. Many people would say that greed dominated during the tech bubble of the late 1990s and fear has ruled behavior in the recent financial crisis. Although true, this characterization is far too simplistic. The human mind is so sophisticated and human emotions are so complex that the emotions of fear and greed do not adequately describe the psychology that affects people as they make investment decisions. This book is one of the first to delve into this fascinating and important subject.

Few other books provide this information because traditional finance has focused on developing the tools that investors use to optimize expected return and risk. This endeavor has been fruitful, yielding tools such as asset pricing models, portfolio theories, and option pricing. Although investors should use these tools in their investment decision making, they typically do not. This is because psychology affects our decisions more than financial theory does.

Unfortunately, psychological biases inhibit one's ability to make good investment decisions. By learning about your psychological biases, you can overcome them and increase your wealth.

You will notice that most of the chapters are structured similarly. A psychological bias is first described and illustrated with everyday behavior (like driving a car). The effect of the bias on investment decisions is then explained. Finally, academic studies are used to show that investors do indeed exhibit the problem.

What we know about investor psychology is increasing rapidly. This fifth edition of *The Psychology of Investing* has a new chapter that describes the psychology involved in the mortgage industry and ensuing financial crisis. New evidence and ideas have been added to every chapter. Every chapter now has a summary, and additional discussion questions have been added.

This material does not replace the investment texts of traditional finance. Understanding psychological biases complements the traditional finance tools. Indeed, after reading this book, you should be convinced that traditional tools are valuable.

NEW TO THIS EDITION

Chapter 1: Psychology and Finance
- Updated the illustrations and financial crisis discussion

Chapter 2: Overconfidence
- Introduced a new subsection "Who Is Overconfident?"
- Added a Summary

Chapter 3: Pride and Regret
- Added a new section "Buying Back Stock Previously Sold"
- Added a new subsection "Reference Point Adaptation"
- Expanded discussion of mutual fund disposition effect

Chapter 4: Risk Perceptions
- Added a new section "Nature or Nurture?"

Chapter 5: Decision Frames
- Added a new subsection on framing in the payday lending industry
- Expanded discussion of IQ and investing
- Included a discussion and illustration of extremeness aversion

Chapter 6: Mental Accounting
- Included a Summary

Chapter 7: Forming Portfolios
- Added a new subsection "Preferred Risk Habitat"
- Added a discussion of the conditional $1/n$ heuristic

Chapter 8: Representativeness and Familiarity
- Added a new subsection "Market Impacts" for the price of home bias with a new figure
- Expanded familiarity with utility stock ownership
- More discussion of investor return chasing

Chapter 9: Social Interaction and Investing
- Added a new subsection "Language" and its influence
- Expanded stale news discussion

Chapter 10: Emotion and Investment Decisions
- Expanded the discussions of the impact of emotions in security pricing, specifically: Ramadan returns and NFL football game returns

Chapter 11: Self-Control and Decision Making
- Added a new subsection on the use of financial advisors

Chapter 12: Psychology in the Mortgage Crisis
- Added a new chapter that describes the psychology involved in the mortgage industry and ensuing financial crisis

COURSESMART

CourseSmart for Instructors

CourseSmart goes beyond traditional expectations by providing instant, online access to the textbooks and course materials you need at a lower cost to students. And, even as students save money, you can save time and hassle with a digital textbook that allows you to search the most relevant content at the very moment you need it. Whether it's evaluating textbooks or creating lecture notes to help students with difficult concepts, CourseSmart can make life a little easier. See how when you visit www.coursesmart.com/instructors.

CourseSmart for Students

CourseSmart goes beyond traditional expectations providing instant, online access to the textbooks and course materials students need at lower cost. They can also search, highlight and take notes anywhere at anytime. See all the benefits to students at www.coursesmart.com/students.

Psychology and Finance

Fear was thick in the air at the start of the financial crisis. The government was clearly worried about a system-wide financial failure. Any observer could see that the people at the Federal Reserve System were frantically throwing unprecedented and dramatic solutions at the problems. They force-fed the largest banks tens of billions of dollars each. They took over other financial institutions like mortgage firms Fannie Mae and Freddie Mac and insurer AIG (American International Group), taking on hundreds of billions more in liabilities.

Through the first three quarters of 2008, the stock market declined 18 percent as measured by the Dow Jones Industrial Average (DJIA). In the fourth quarter, during the panic, the market lost another 19 percent. The losses accelerated in the first quarter of 2009. The market declined 25 percent to a low on March 5, 2009. Of course, investors did not know that was the bottom. All they knew was that the market had declined for over a year and by a total of more than 50 percent. In addition, the losses had been most dramatic recently. What were individual investors doing during this time? They were selling stocks. They sold more than $150 billion of stock mutual funds these last two quarters. Much of this was at or near the market bottom. As a comparison, the same investors were net buyers of $11 billion in stock mutual funds during the month of the market top. Even into 2012, individual investors were not buying into the stock market like they did before. Once bit, twice shy?

Intellectually, we all know that we need to buy low and sell high in order to make money in stocks. Yet as these numbers illustrate, individual investors are notoriously bad market timers. Our psychological biases are particularly destructive during times of large market swings because emotions get magnified.

But it wasn't just individual investors' cognitive biases that were exposed during this time of economic turmoil; the errors of finance professionals were also laid bare. These corporate and institutional investors tend to create elaborate models in an attempt to describe all the factors impacting investment prices. Over time, they become too reliant on these models. Their overconfidence leads to greater risk taking. At some point, and unbeknownst to them, they have risked the life of their firm. Then the unexpected occurs. Nassim Taleb calls it a *Black Swan*—after the European assumption that all swans were white—that is, until they went to Australia and much to their surprise, found black swans. This time, the rare and important event was that U.S. housing prices started to decline and people started defaulting on their mortgages.

Many financial institutions found that in their hubris, they had over leveraged themselves and were quickly sinking. Hundreds of banks failed. Investment banks were liquidated or experienced a forced sale. Large commercial banks were bailed out by the government. Hedge funds were liquidated. Finance professionals had bet their firms and their careers on their models and lost.

Why do investors and finance professionals frequently make poor decisions? Although some people may be ill informed or poorly trained, these mistakes are often made by highly intelligent and well-trained individuals. All of these problems stem from cognitive errors, psychological biases, and emotions. These problems are not discussed in traditional finance education. These topics are described in what is known as *behavioral finance*.

TRADITIONAL VERSUS BEHAVIORAL FINANCE

Historically, a formal education in finance has dismissed the idea that one's personal psychology can be a detriment in making good investment decisions. For the past three decades, the field of finance has evolved based on the following two assumptions:

- People make rational decisions.
- People are unbiased in their predictions about the future.

By assuming that people act in their own best interests, the finance field has been able to create some powerful tools for investors. For example, investors can use modern portfolio theory to obtain the highest expected return possible for any given level of risk they can bear. Pricing models (such as the capital asset pricing model, the arbitrage pricing theory, and option pricing) can help value securities and provide insights into expected risks and returns. Investment texts are full of these useful theories.

However, psychologists have known for a long time that these are bad assumptions. People often act in a seemingly irrational manner and make predictable errors in their forecasts. For example, traditional finance assumes that people are risk averse. They prefer not to take risk but will do so if the expected rewards are sufficient. People should also be consistent in their level of risk aversion. But in the real world, people's behaviors routinely violate these assumptions. For instance, people exhibit risk aversion when buying insurance and simultaneously exhibit a risk-seeking behavior when buying lottery tickets.

The finance field has been slow to accept the possibility that economic decisions could be predictably biased. Early proponents of behavioral finance often were considered heretics. Over the past decade though, the evidence that psychology and emotions influence financial decisions became more convincing. Today, the early proponents of behavioral finance are no longer heretics but visionaries. Although the controversies of when, how, and why psychology affects investing continue, many believe that the 2002 Nobel Prize in Economics awarded to psychologist Daniel Kahneman and experimental economist Vernon Smith has vindicated the field.

Financial economists are now realizing that investors can be irrational. Indeed, predictable decision errors by investors can affect the function of the markets. The contributions of behavioral finance include (1) documenting actual investor behavior, (2) documenting price patterns that seem inconsistent with traditional models with rational investors, and (3) providing new theories to explain these behaviors and patterns.[1]

Perhaps most important, people's reasoning errors affect their investing and ultimately their wealth. Investors who understand the tools of modern investing still can fail as investors if they let psychological biases control their decisions. By reading this book, you will:

- learn many psychological biases that affect decision making,
- understand how these biases affect investment decisions,
- see how these decisions reduce your wealth, and
- learn to recognize and avoid them in your own life.

The rest of this chapter will illustrate that these psychological problems are real. The arguments will be far more convincing if you participate in the following demonstration.

PREDICTION

The brain does not work like a computer. Instead, it frequently processes information through shortcuts and emotional filters to shorten analysis time. The decision arrived at through this process is often not the same decision you would make without these filters. These filters and shortcuts can be referred to as psychological biases. Knowing about these psychological biases is the first step toward avoiding them. One common problem is overestimating the precision and importance of information. The following demonstration illustrates this problem.

Let's face it; investing is difficult. You must make decisions based on information that might be inadequate or inaccurate. Additionally, you must understand and analyze the information effectively. Unfortunately, people make predictable errors in their forecasts.

Consider the 10 questions in Table 1.1.[2] Although you probably do not know the answers to these questions, enter the most probable range based on your best estimate. Specifically, give your best low guess and your best high guess so that you are 90 percent sure the answer lies somewhere between the two. Don't make the range so wide that the answer is guaranteed to lie within

TABLE 1.1   Enter the Range (Minimum and Maximum) for Which You Are 90 Percent Certain the Answer Lies Within

	Min	Max
1. What is the average weight, in pounds, of the adult blue whale?	___	___
2. In what year was the Mona Lisa painted by Leonardo da Vinci?	___	___
3. How many independent countries were members of the United Nations in 2012?	___	___
4. What is the air distance, in miles, between Paris, France, and Sydney, Australia?	___	___
5. How many bones are in the human body?	___	___
6. How many total combatants were killed in World War I?	___	___
7. How many items (books, manuscripts, microforms, sheet music, etc.) were listed in the U.S. Library of Congress at the end of 2010?	___	___
8. How long, in miles, is the Amazon River?	___	___
9. How fast does the earth spin (miles per hour) at the equator?	___	___
10. How many earthquakes per year does the National Earthquake Information Center locate and publish information about, globally?	___	___
	___	___

the range, and also don't make the range too narrow. If you consistently choose a range following these instructions, you should expect to get nine of the ten questions correct. Go ahead, give it your best shot.

If you have no idea of the answer to a question, then your range should be wide for you to be 90 percent confident. On the other hand, if you think you can give a good educated guess, then you can choose a smaller range to be 90 percent confident. Now let's check the answers. They are (1) 250,000 pounds; (2) 1505; (3) 193 countries; (4) 10,543 miles; (5) 206 bones; (6) 8.3 million; (7) 147 million items; (8) 4,000 miles; (9) 1,044 miles per hour; and (10) 20,000. Count your response correct if the answer lies between your low and high guesses. How many did you get right?

Most people miss five or more questions. However, if you are 90 percent sure of your range, then you should have missed only one. The fact is that you are too certain about your answers, even when you have no information or knowledge about the topic. Even being educated in probability is of no help. Most finance professors miss at least five of the questions, too.

This demonstration illustrates that people have difficulty evaluating the precision of their knowledge and information. Now that you see the difficulty, you can have a chance to redeem yourself. Because this book relates psychology to investing, consider the following question:

In 1928, the modern era of the Dow Jones Industrial Average (DJIA) began as it expanded to 30 stocks. In 1929, the index started the year at 300. At the end of 2011, the DJIA was at 12,218. The DJIA is a price-weighted average. Dividends are omitted from the index. What would the DJIA average have been at the end of 2011 if the dividends were reinvested each year?

Notice that Table 1.1 has room for your DJIA minimum and maximum guesses. Again, you should be 90 percent sure that the correct value lies within the range you choose.

Because you are 90 percent sure that the correct value lies within the range you chose, you should get this one correct. Are you ready for the answer? If dividends were reinvested in the DJIA, the average would have been 332,130 at the end of 2011.[3] Does this surprise you? Does it seem impossible? Let me reframe the problem from prices to returns. Using my financial calculator, I find that the average annual return of 300 growing to 332,130 over 83 years is 8.81 percent. Does a nearly 9 percent average return in the stock market seem reasonable? Even after learning that most people set their prediction range too narrowly and experiencing the problem firsthand, most people continue to do it. Also notice how important is the framing of the problem.

This example also illustrates another aspect of investor psychology called *anchoring*. When you read the question, you focused on the DJIA price level of 12,218; that is, you anchored your thinking to 12,218. You probably made your guess by starting at this anchor and then trying to add an appropriate amount to compensate for the dividends. Investors anchor on their stock purchase price and the recent highest stock price.

BEHAVIORAL FINANCE

Even the smartest people are affected by psychological biases, but traditional finance has considered this irrelevant. Traditional finance assumes that people are "rational" and tells us how people should behave in order to maximize their wealth. These ideas have brought us arbitrage theory, portfolio theory, asset pricing theory, and option pricing theory.

Alternatively, behavioral finance studies how people actually behave in a financial setting.[4] Specifically, it is the study of how emotions and cognitive biases affect financial decisions, corporations, and the financial markets. This book focuses on a subset of these issues—how psychological biases affect investors. The investor who truly understands these biases will also appreciate more fully the tools traditional finance has provided.

To begin, consider the decision-making process shown in Figure 1.1. In order to evaluate a decision that includes risk and/or uncertainty, the brain uses inputs like the facts of the situation and probability estimates to attempt to quantify the uncertainties. However, both the current mood and the anticipated feelings about the result of the decision also become inputs. It should be no surprise that when emotions get involved in the process, biased decisions often result. We often think of this part of the process as being more computer-like. Possibly more interesting is that the "computer-like" part of the cognitive process (i.e., the reason, or logic, portion of the brain) also yields systematic and

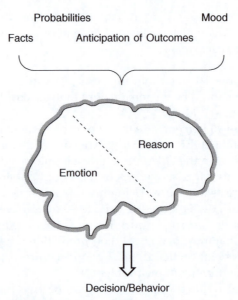

Probabilities   Mood

Facts   Anticipation of Outcomes

Reason

Emotion

Decision/Behavior

FIGURE 1.1   Decision-Making Process

predictable cognitive errors. Thus, decisions and the results of those decisions are often biased no matter whether emotion plays a role.

SOURCES OF COGNITIVE ERRORS

Many of the behaviors of investors are outcomes of *prospect theory*. This theory describes how people frame and value a decision involving uncertainty.[5] First, investors frame the choices in terms of potential gains and losses relative to a specific reference point. Framing is a common and pervasive behavior that has a strong ability to influence opinions and decisions. (See Chapter 5.) Although investors seem to anchor on various reference points, the purchase price appears to be important. Second, investors value the gains/losses according to an *S*-shaped function as shown in Figure 1.2.

Notice several things about the value function in the figure. First, the function is concave for gains. Investors feel good (i.e., have higher utility) when they make a $500 gain. They feel better when they make a $1,000 gain. However, they do not feel twice as good when they gain $1,000 as when they gain $500.

Second, notice that the function is convex for taking a loss. This means that investors feel bad when they have a loss, but twice the loss does not make them feel twice as bad.

Third, the function is steeper for losses than for gains. This asymmetry between gains and losses leads to different reactions in dealing with winning and losing positions. (See Chapter 3.)

An additional aspect of prospect theory is that people segregate each investment in order to track gains and losses and periodically reexamine positions. These separate accounts are referred to as *mental accounting*.[6]

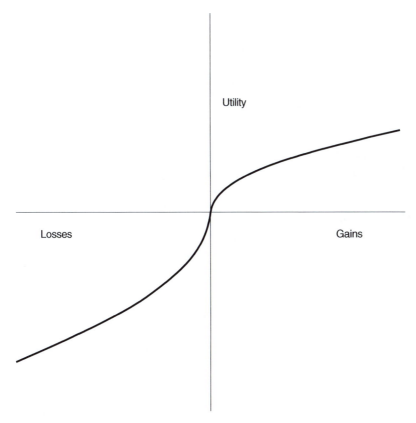

Utility

Losses   Gains

FIGURE 1.2   Prospect Theory Value Function

(See Chapter 6.) Viewing each investment separately rather than using a portfolio approach limits investors' ability to minimize risk and maximize return. (See Chapter 7.)

A different approach to the psychology of investing is to categorize be-havioral biases by their source.[7] Some cognitive errors result from *self-deception*, which occurs because people tend to think they are better than they really are. This self-deception helps them fool others and thus survive the natural selec-tion process. Another source of bias comes from *heuristic simplification*. Simply stated, heuristic simplification exists because constraints on cognitive resources (like memory, attention, and processing power) force the brain to shortcut com-plex analyses. Prospect theory is considered an outcome of heuristic simplifica-tion. A third source of bias comes from a person's *mood*, which can overcome reason.

Human interaction and peer effects are also important in financial decision making. Human interactions are how people share information and communi-cate feelings about the information. The cues obtained about the opinions and emotions of others influence one's decisions.

BIAS AND WEALTH IMPACT

This book demonstrates how psychological biases, cognitive errors, and emotions affect investor decisions. It also shows the wealth ramifications of these biased decisions. In other words, not only do people make predictable errors, but those errors cost them financially. The primary goal of this book is to help you understand and control the biases in yourself and those with whom you interact. In addition, some readers may find opportunities to financially benefit from the biased decisions of other investors.

As an example, consider that people place too much emphasis on the few observations they have witnessed to make predictions about future outcomes. First, consider the three outcomes of flipping a coin, head, head, and head. We know that we should expect there to be equal numbers of heads and tails in the long run. Observing an imbalance like three heads leads people to behave as if there is a greater chance of a tail on the next flip. Since we know the underlying distribution (50 percent chance of heads, 50 percent chance of tails), we tend to believe in a correction. This is known as the *gambler's fallacy* and is part of a larger misunderstanding referred to as the *law of small numbers*.[8]

Consider how this behavior impacts those who play the lottery. In the long run, people know that each number in a lottery should be picked an equal number of times. So they tend to avoid numbers that have been recently picked because it seems less likely that they should be picked again so soon. So this fallacy biases people toward picking lottery numbers that have not been picked in a while. You might ask how this impacts their wealth; after all, the numbers they pick are as equally likely to be chosen as any others. Say that everyone who plays the lottery (except me) avoids the numbers that have recently been picked. I select the recent numbers. Remember that lottery jackpots are split between all the winners. If my numbers get chosen in the lottery, I am the only winner and get to keep the entire jackpot. If you are the winner, you are likely to split with others and thus receive only a small share of the jackpot. Our probabilities of winning are the same, but by following the crowd of people suffering from gambler's fallacy, you would have a smaller expected payoff. Notice that by understanding this bias, I am able to change my decisions to avoid it and better position myself to make more money than those who suffer from it.

Belief in the law of small numbers causes people to behave a little differently in the stock market. With coins and lotteries, we believe that we understand the underlying distribution of outcomes. But we don't know the underlying distribution of outcomes for different stocks and mutual funds. In fact, we believe that some stocks and mutual funds are better than others. Here we take the small number of observations we see as representative of what to expect in the future. Unusual success is believed to continue. When people believe they understand the underlying distribution of outcomes, they predict unusual occurrences to reverse. Alternatively, when they do not know the underlying distribution, they predict unusual performance to continue. We thus see investors "chase" last year's high-performing mutual funds.

WHAT TO EXPECT

The next seven chapters of this book discuss psychological biases that affect people's daily lives. These chapters are all structured in a similar manner. First, the psychological trait is identified and explained using common, daily activities as examples. Second, the results of research studies show how the bias affects real people. Last, the degree to which investors are affected by the bias is examined.

Chapters 2 through 4 demonstrate how investment decision making is affected by emotions and framing. As illustrated in the previous example, people set their range of possible outcomes too narrowly. This is part of a self-deception problem called *overconfidence*. Overconfident investors trade too much, take too much risk, and earn lower returns. This topic is discussed in Chapter 2. Chapter 3 illustrates how investors' views of themselves cause them to avoid feelings of regret and instead seek pride. Consequently, investors sell winner stocks too soon and hold on to loser stocks too long. Last, Chapter 4 demonstrates investors' perceptions of risk and how they change from time to time and from analysis to analysis. This changing risk behavior has a dramatic impact on the decision-making process. Indeed, your memory of the past might change over time to soften your regret over failures.

Chapters 5 through 8 demonstrate how heuristic simplification affects the investor. For example, even feeling whether a stock you hold is a winner or loser involves *framing* (Chapter 5). Consider that you bought a stock for $30 five years ago. That stock rose to $60 last year, but now is at only $45. Do you consider this stock to be a winner or a loser for you? Your decision on this frame will lead you to specific holding or selling behaviors. Now consider that every day you are bombarded by information; the brain uses a process called *mental accounting* to store and keep track of important decisions and outcomes.

Chapter 6 shows that people make poor financial decisions as a consequence of this process. Discussed in Chapter 7 is one particularly important implication—how investors view portfolio diversification. The brain also uses shortcuts to process information quickly. These shortcuts create a tainted view of the information. This leads to the problems of representativeness and familiarity for the investor. These problems are discussed in Chapter 8.

The last three chapters are a little different. Chapter 9 discusses how investing has entered our social culture. The interaction among psychology, group psychology, and investing can contribute to market mania and price bubbles. The Internet also interacts with these factors to magnify the psychological biases. This is important because investors are influenced by the decisions being made around them. Chapter 10 focuses on the role of emotions and mood in the decision-making process. An investor's general level of optimism or pessimism influences his or her trading decisions. Chapter 11 discusses the difficulty of maintaining self-control in the face of these psychological biases. Planning, incentives, and rules of thumb are helpful in avoiding common problems. This chapter also describes programs (like Save More Tomorrow and Save to Win) that are designed using people's biases to help them save more. Lastly, Chapter 12 illustrates the role psychology played in the mortgage industry and ensuing financial crisis. Predatory lenders created subprime mortgages that would hide their high costs in low salient dimensions and targeted emotionally stressed homeowners.

Summary

Most formal finance education centers on traditional finance concepts. However, psychology plays a large role in financial decision making. This book demonstrates how cognitive errors, heuristics, psychological biases, and emotions influence an investor's decisions. Unfortunately, these psychology-induced decisions create outcomes that often have negative impacts on wealth.

Questions

1. Why might the traditional assumption of rational decision making make sense for investors?
2. Name four aspects of prospect theory.
3. Describe three sources of cognitive errors other than prospect theory.
4. How do emotions and moods contribute to a person's decision-making process?

Notes

1. For a discussion, see Annette Vissing-Jorgensen, "Perspectives on Behavioral Finance: Does 'Irrationality' Disappear with Wealth? Evidence from Expectations and Actions," *NBER Macroeconomics Annual* 18(2003): 139–194.
2. This exercise is similar to one proposed by Edward Russo and Paul Shoemaker in *Decision Traps* (New York: Simon & Schuster, 1989) and a presentation by Hersh Shefrin at the 2000 Financial Management Association annual meeting.
3. This is an extension of the analysis done in Roger Clarke and Meir Statman, "The DJIA Crossed 652,230," *Journal of Portfolio Management* (Winter 2000): 89–93.
4. See the discussion in Meir Statman, "Behavioral Finance: Past Battles and Future Engagements," *Financial Analysts Journal* (November/December 1999): 18–27. I use the term *traditional finance* where Meir uses the term *standard finance*.
5. See Daniel Kahneman and Amos Tversky, "Prospect Theory: An Analysis of Decision under Risk," *Econometrica* 46(1979): 171–185.
6. See Richard Thaler, "Mental Accounting and Consumer Choice," *Marketing Science* 4(1985): 199–214.
7. See David Hirshleifer, "Investor Psychology and Asset Pricing," *Journal of Finance* 56(2001): 1533–1597.
8. See Matthew Rabin, "Inference by Believers in the Law of Small Numbers," *Quarterly Journal of Economics* 117(2002): 775–816.

Overconfidence

People can be overconfident. Psychologists have determined that overconfidence causes people to overestimate their knowledge, underestimate risks, and exaggerate their ability to control events. Does overconfidence occur in investment decision making? Security selection is a difficult task. It is precisely in this type of task that people exhibit the greatest degree of overconfidence.

There are two aspects to overconfidence: miscalibration and the better-than-average effect. The miscalibration facet is that people's probability distributions are too tight. The illustration in Chapter 1 using the 10 questions and 90 percent range responses is an example of miscalibration. The better-than-average effect simply means that people have unrealistically positive views of themselves. They believe that their abilities, knowledge, and skills are better than the average person's. An illustration of this effect is the answer to the following question:

> *Are you a good driver? Compared to the drivers you encounter on the road, are you above average, average, or below average?*

How did you answer this question? If overconfidence were not involved, approximately one-third of you would answer *above average*, one-third would say *average*, and one-third would say *below average*. However, people are overconfident of their abilities. In one published study, 82 percent of the sampled college students rated themselves above average in driving ability.[1] Clearly, many of them are mistaken.

Many of those students were mistaken because they were overconfident about their driving skills. Being overconfident about driving skills might not be a problem that affects your life, but people are overconfident about their skills in many things. This overconfidence can even affect your financial future.

Consider this financially oriented example. Starting a business is a risky venture; in fact, most new businesses fail. When 2,994 new business owners were asked about their chances of success, they thought they had a 70 percent chance of success, but only 39 percent thought that any business like theirs would be as likely to succeed.[2] Why do new business owners think they have nearly twice the chance of success as others? They are overconfident.

Interestingly, people are more overconfident when they feel they have control over the outcome—even when this is clearly not the case. For example, it is documented that if people are asked to bet on whether the result of a coin toss will be heads or tails, most bet larger amounts if the coin is yet to be tossed. That is, if the coin is tossed and the outcome is concealed, people will offer lower amounts when asked for bets. On the other hand, if asked for a bet before the toss, people tend to bet higher amounts. People act as if their involvement will somehow affect the outcome of the toss.[3] In this case, control of the outcome is clearly an illusion. This perception occurs in investing as well. Even without information, people believe the stocks they own will perform better than the stocks they do not own. However, ownership of a stock only gives the illusion of having control over the performance of the stock.

A Gallup/Paine Webber survey of individual investors conducted in early 2001 demonstrates this overconfidence. Of particular note is that many of those surveyed had recently experienced some negative outcomes after the technology stock bubble collapsed. When asked what they thought the stock market return would be during the next 12 months, the average answer was 10.3 percent. When asked what return they expected to earn on their portfolios, the average response was 11.7 percent. Typically, investors expect to earn an above-average return.

OVERCONFIDENCE AFFECTS INVESTOR DECISIONS

Investing is a difficult process. It entails gathering information, analyzing it, and making a decision based on that information. However, overconfidence causes us to misinterpret the accuracy of our information and overestimate our skill in analyzing it. It occurs after we experience some success. The *self-attribution* bias leads people to believe that successes are attributed to skill while failure is caused by bad luck. After some success in the market, investors may exhibit overconfident behavior.

Consider the behavior of financial analysts. Analysts publicize their predictions about the future earnings of the firms they follow. Gilles Hilary and Lior Menzly studied the predictions of analysts after the analysts have shown a series of good earnings estimates.[4] If this success causes the analysts to put excessive weight on their private information and skill, then their next predictions are likely to be less accurate than average and deviate from the other analysts. After examining over 40,000 quarterly earnings predictions, Hilary and Menzly found that success leads to overconfidence. Analysts who perform well for a few quarters follow with predictions that are different from other analysts' estimates and ultimately have greater errors.

Overconfidence can lead investors to poor trading decisions, which often manifest themselves as excessive trading, risk taking, and ultimately portfolio losses. Their overconfidence increases the amount they trade because it causes them to be too certain about their opinions. Investors' opinions are derived from their beliefs regarding the accuracy of the information they have obtained and their ability to interpret it.[5] Overconfident investors believe more strongly in their own valuation of a stock and concern themselves less about the beliefs of others.

Overconfident Trading

Psychologists have found that men are more overconfident than women in tasks perceived to fall into the masculine domain, such as managing finances.[6] Men generally are more overconfident about their ability to make investment decisions than women are; therefore, male investors trade more frequently than female investors do.

Two financial economists, Brad Barber and Terrance Odean, examined the trading behavior of nearly 38,000 households of a large discount brokerage firm between 1991 and 1997.[7] They examined the level of trading in brokerage accounts owned by single and married men and women. A common measure for the level of trading is called *turnover*. Turnover is the percentage of stocks in the portfolio that changed during the year. For example, a 50 percent turnover during a year is the equivalent to an investor selling half the stocks in a portfolio during that year and purchasing new stocks. Similarly, a 200 percent turnover is equivalent to an investor selling all the stocks in the portfolio to purchase others, then selling those stocks to purchase a third set during one year's time.

The study shows that single men trade the most. As illustrated in Figure 2.1, single men trade at a rate equivalent to an 85 percent annual turnover. This compares with an annual turnover of 73 percent for married men. Married and single women trade only the equivalent of 53 percent and 51 percent in annual turnover, respectively. Note that this is consistent with overconfidence; that is, male investors are more overconfident than female investors, leading to higher levels of trading.

On the other hand, it is possible that men are not overconfident but rather that they might be better informed. If you truly have better information, trading based on that information should lead to achieving higher returns.

In general, overconfident investors trade more—but is higher turnover and increased trading bad? Barber and Odean also explore this issue.[8] In a sample of 78,000 household accounts over the period 1991–1996, they examined the relationship between turnover and portfolio returns. Consider an investor who receives accurate information and is highly capable of interpreting it. The investor's high frequency of trading should result in high returns due to the individual's skill and the quality of the information. In fact, these returns should be high enough to beat a simple buy-and-hold strategy while covering the costs of trading. On the other hand, if the investor does not have superior ability but rather is suffering from a dose of overconfidence, then the high frequency of turnover will not result in portfolio returns large enough to beat the buy-and-hold strategy and cover costs.

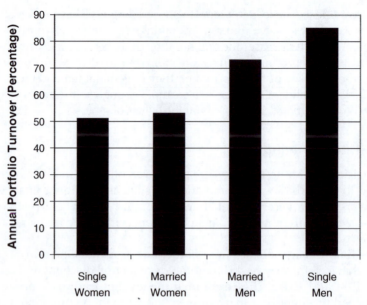

FIGURE 2.1   Annual Portfolio Turnover by Gender and Marital Status

Barber and Odean determined the level of trading for the investors in their sample and categorized them into five groups. The first 20 percent of investors, with the lowest turnover rate, were placed in the first group. On average, this group turned over their portfolio at a rate of 2.4 percent per year. The 20 percent of investors with the next-lowest turnover rate were placed in the second group. This process continued until the investors with the highest turnover rate were placed in the fifth (and last) group. This high-turnover rate group had an average annual turnover rate of more than 250 percent per year.

Figure 2.2 reports the average annual return for each of the five groups. Note that all five groups earned the same 18.7 percent annually in gross returns. Therefore, high-turnover investors did not realize higher returns for their additional efforts. However, commissions must be paid for buying and selling stocks. This has a greater effect on the investors who trade more frequently, as illustrated in the figure. Net returns (returns after commission costs) to the investor are much lower for the high-turnover group. The net returns for the lowest-turnover group average 18.5 percent per year versus 11.4 percent for the highest-turnover group.

The net difference of 7 percent per year between the highest- and lowest-turnover groups is dramatic. For example, if the investors in the lowest-turnover group invest $10,000 over five years, earning 18.5 percent per year, they will have $23,366. If the investors in the highest-turnover group invest the same amount and receive 11.4 percent per year, they can expect only $17,156—a difference of more than $5,000. Overconfidence-based trading is hazardous when it comes to accumulating wealth.

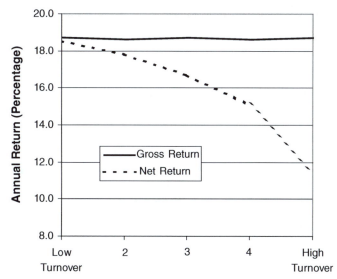

FIGURE 2.2   Annual Return of Investors Sorted by Portfolio Turnover

High commission costs are not the only problem caused by excessive trading. It has been observed that overconfidence leads to trading too frequently as well as to purchasing the wrong stocks. Barber and Odean limited their analysis to a sample of brokerage accounts that had complete liquidations of a stock followed by the purchase of a different stock within three weeks. Then they followed the performance of the stocks sold and purchased over the subsequent four months and one year.

They wanted to determine whether selling stock A and purchasing stock B typically was a good decision. Apparently not. The stocks that investors sold earned 2.6 percent during the following four months, whereas the replacement stocks earned only 0.11 percent. In the year following the trades, stocks that had been sold outperformed stocks purchased by 5.8 percent.[9] Not only does overconfidence cause you to trade too much and burn money on commissions, it can also cause you to sell a good-performing stock in order to purchase a poor one.

One criticism of the Barber and Odean studies is that they essentially assume that high-volume traders are overconfident. In other words, they use trading volume as an indication of overconfidence. However, does overconfidence really cause overtrading? Markus Glaser and Martin Weber examined this question by studying investors at an online German brokerage.[10] They surveyed the investors by asking questions to assess their level of overconfidence. For example, they asked questions like "What percentage of the customers of your brokerage have better skills than you in identifying stocks with above-average return prospects?" Since the authors had the investors' past portfolio positions and trading records, they could assess whether the investors really were better skilled. Interestingly, they found no correlation between investors' answers and historical differences in performance. They found, however, that this better-than-average measure of overconfidence is positively related to trading volume. Overconfident investors did trade more.

Overconfidence and the Market

If many investors suffer from overconfidence at the same time, then signs reflecting such a trend might be found within the stock market. While the excessive trading of overconfident investors has been identified through brokerage accounts, does this behavior show up in the aggregate market? Several researchers believe that it does. Specifically, after the overall stock market increases, many investors may attribute their success to their own skill and become overconfident. This will lead to greater trading by a large group of investors and may impact overall trading volume on the stock exchanges.

Examining monthly stock market returns and trading volume over 40 years shows that higher volume does follow months with high returns.[11] For example, a relatively high return of 7 percent one month is associated with higher trading during the following six months. The extra trading represents seven months of normal trading squeezed into six months. Alternatively, overall trading is lower after market declines. Investors appear to attribute the success of a good month to their own skill and begin trading more. Poor performance makes them less overconfident and is followed by lower trading activity. This may be why the old Wall Street adage warns investors not to confuse brains with a bull market!

OVERCONFIDENCE AND RISK

Overconfidence also affects investors' risk-taking behavior. Rational investors try to maximize returns while minimizing the amount of risk taken. However, overconfident investors misinterpret the level of risk they take. After all, if an investor is confident that the stocks picked will have a high return, then where is the risk?

The portfolios of overconfident investors will have higher risk for two reasons. First is the tendency to purchase higher-risk stocks. Higher-risk stocks are generally from smaller, newer companies. The second reason is a tendency to underdiversify their portfolios. Prevalent risk can be measured in several ways: portfolio volatility, beta, and the size of the firms in the portfolio. Portfolio volatility measures the degree of ups and downs the portfolio experiences. High-volatility portfolios exhibit dramatic swings in price and are indicative of underdiversification. Beta is a variable commonly used in the investment industry to measure the riskiness of a security. It measures the degree a portfolio changes with the stock market. A beta of 1 indicates that the portfolio closely follows the swings of the market. A higher beta indicates that the security has higher risk and will exhibit more volatility than the stock market in general.

The series of studies by Barber and Odean show that overconfident investors take more risks. They found that single men have the highest-risk portfolios followed by married men, married women, and single women. That is, the portfolios of single men have the highest volatility and the highest beta and tend to include the stocks of smaller companies. Among the five groups of investors sorted by turnover, the high-turnover group invested in stocks of smaller firms with higher betas compared with the stocks of the low-turnover group. Overall, overconfident investors perceive their actions to be less risky than generally proves to be the case.

ILLUSION OF KNOWLEDGE

Where does overconfidence come from? It comes partially from the illusion of knowledge. This refers to the tendency for people to believe that the accuracy of their forecasts increases with more information; that is, more information increases one's knowledge about something and improves one's decisions.[12]

However, this is not always the case. For example, if I roll a fair, six-sided die, what number do you think will come up, and how sure are you that you are right? Clearly, you can pick any number between 1 and 6 and have a one-sixth chance of being right. Now let me tell you that the last three rolls of the die have each produced the number 4. I will roll the die again. What number do you think will come up, and what is your chance of being right? If the die is truly fair, then you could still pick any number between 1 and 6 and have a one-sixth chance of being correct. The added information does not increase your ability to forecast the roll of the die. However, many people believe the number 4 has a greater chance (more than one-sixth) of being rolled again. Others believe the number 4 has a lower chance of being rolled again. These people think their chance of being right is higher than reality. That is, the new information makes people more confident of their predictions even though their chances for being correct do not change.

Although valuable information may improve prediction accuracy, it may increase confidence at a faster rate than accuracy. In other words, receiving more and better information causes one's confidence in making predictions to jump quickly while that information only marginally improves accuracy, if at all. A series of experiments trying to predict college football game outcomes illustrates this effect.[13] Participants were given some statistical information (but no team names) and asked to predict the winner and a point-spread range. They also assessed their own probability of being right. When more information about the game was provided, participants updated their predictions and self-assessments. Five blocks of information were eventually given for each game and each participant predicted 15 games. The results show that prediction accuracy did not improve as more blocks of information were given. There was an accuracy of 64 percent with only one block of information and that increased to only 66 percent will all five blocks of information. On the other hand, confidence started at 69 percent and increased to 79 percent with all the information. In another experiment, these researchers ordered the quality of information blocks. Some participants saw the quality of information improve with the revelation of each new block, while the other participants started with the best information and then saw blocks that became less valuable. The results are the same: People became more confident as they received more information, even though the accuracy of their predictions did not improve.

Using the Internet, investors have access to vast quantities of information. This information includes historical data such as past prices, returns, and firm operational performance as well as current information such as real-time news, prices, and volume. However, most individual investors lack the training and experience of professional investors and therefore are less sure of how to interpret the information. That is, this information does not give them as much knowledge about the situation as they think because they do not have the training to interpret it properly. This is the difference between knowledge and wisdom.

A good example is to illustrate the kind of information investors might use to make decisions. Consider the distinction between unfiltered information and filtered information. The unfiltered information comes directly from the source, like company financial statements. This information can be difficult to understand because it is riddled with jargon and complicated accounting rules. Filtered information is unfiltered data that is interpreted and packaged by professionals for general investor consumption, like information from analysts or services like Value Line. It is easy and cheap for novice investors to collect unfiltered information. Yet, it is likely that these inexperienced investors may be fooled by the illusion of knowledge and make poor decisions because of their failure to properly understand the unfiltered information. They would be better off using filtered information until they gain more experience. One financial study examined the types of information, experience, and portfolio returns of investors. The study confirmed that lower returns occur for less-experienced investors when they rely more on unfiltered information. Relying on filtered information improved returns for these investors.[14] More experienced investors can achieve higher returns using unfiltered information. Presumably, experience helps them turn knowledge into wisdom.

Many individual investors realize they have a limited ability to interpret investment information, so they use the Internet for help. Investors can get analyst recommendations, subscribe to expert services, join newsgroups, and learn others' opinions through chat rooms and Web postings. However, online investors need to take what they see in these chat rooms with a grain of salt. Not all recommendations are from experts.

In fact, few chat-room recommendations may be from experts. A recent study examined the stocks recommended by people who posted messages on the boards of two Internet newsgroups.[15] Most of the stocks recommended had recently performed very well or very poorly. The stocks with very good performance the previous month were recommended as a purchase (momentum strategy). These stocks subsequently underperformed the market by more than 19 percent the next month. The stocks with extremely poor performance during the previous month that were recommended for purchase (value strategy) outperformed the market by more than 25 percent over the following month. Overall, the stocks recommended for purchase did not perform significantly better or worse than the market in general.

Another study finds that positive message board postings at Raging Bull.com are not associated with positive stock returns the following day or week.[16] However, unusually high numbers of postings are associated with higher trading volume. These studies conclude that message board stock recommendations do not contain valuable information for investors. However, if investors perceive the messages as having increased their knowledge, they might be overconfident about their investment decisions. The higher trading volume indicates that this might be the case.

Who Is Overconfident?

We often think of two kinds of investors in the stock market—individual investors and institutional investors. Which type is more prone to overconfidence? Two scholars, Chuang and Susmel, compare the trading activity of both types of investors on the Taiwanese stock market.[17] They specifically look at market conditions that foster overconfident trading, like after the gains of a bull market or after large gains in individual stocks.

While both individual and institutional investors exhibit higher trading activities during these likely overconfident periods, the effect is greater for individual investors. Also, while trading more during these periods of likely overconfidence, individual investors also shift to more risky stocks. The combination of both higher trading and greater risk taking by individuals after market gains suggest that they are prone to overconfidence. Not only do individual investors trade more aggressively aftermarket gains, but their performance gets worse than the institutional investors.

ILLUSION OF CONTROL

Another important psychological factor is the illusion of control. People often believe they have influence over the outcome of uncontrollable events. The key attributes that foster the illusion of control are choice, outcome sequence, task familiarity, information, and active involvement.[18] Online investors routinely experience these attributes.

Choice

Making an active choice induces control. For example, people who choose their own lottery numbers believe they have a better chance of winning than people who have numbers given to them at random. Because online brokers do not provide advice to investors, investors must make their own choices regarding what (and when) to buy and sell.

Outcome Sequence

The way in which an outcome occurs affects the illusion of control. Early positive outcomes give the person a greater illusion of control than early negative outcomes do. Investors were getting on the Web during the late 1990s and taking control of their investments, and because this period was an extended bull market interval, they likely experienced many positive outcomes.

Task Familiarity

The more familiar people are with a task, the more they feel in control of the task. As discussed later in this chapter, investors have been becoming familiar with the online investment environment and have been active traders and participants in Web information services.

Information

When a greater amount of information is obtained, the illusion of control is greater as well. The vast amount of information on the Internet already has been illustrated.

Active Involvement

When a person participates a great deal in a task, the feeling of being in control is also proportionately greater. Online investors have high participation rates in the investment process. Investors using discount brokers (such as online brokers) must devise their own investment decision-making process. These investors obtain and evaluate information, make trading decisions, and place the trades.

The Internet fosters further active involvement by providing the medium for investment chat rooms, message boards, and newsgroups. Internet investment services firms such as Yahoo!, Motley Fool, Silicon Investor, and The Raging Bull sponsor message boards on their Web sites where investors can communicate with each other. Typically, message boards are available for each stock listed on the exchange. Users post a message about a firm using an alias or simply read the message postings.

Past Successes

Overconfidence is learned through past success. If a decision turns out to be good, then it is attributed to skill and ability. If a decision turns out to be bad, then it is attributed to bad luck. The more successes people experience, the more they will attribute it to their own ability, even when much luck is involved.

During bull markets, individual investors will attribute too much of their success to their own abilities, which makes them overconfident. As a consequence, overconfident behaviors (e.g., high levels of trading and risk taking) will be more pronounced in bull markets than in bear markets.[19]

This is borne out in the behavior of investors during the bull market of the late 1990s and the subsequent bear market. As the bull market raged on, individual investors traded more than ever. In addition, investors allocated higher proportions of their assets to stocks, invested in riskier companies, and even leveraged their positions by using more margin (borrowed money).[20] These behaviors slowly became reversed as the overconfidence of the people investing in the bull market faded and the bear market dragged on.

ONLINE TRADING

Brad Barber and Terrance Odean investigated the trading behavior of 1,607 investors who switched from a phone-based trading system to an Internet-based trading system at a discount brokerage firm.[21] In the two years prior to the time investors went online, the average portfolio turnover was about 70 percent. After going online, the trading of these investors immediately jumped to a turnover of 120 percent. Some of this increase is transitory; however, the turnover rate of these investors was still 90 percent two years after going online.

A different study investigated the effect of Web-based trading in 401(k) pension plans.[22] A total of 100,000 plan participants from two companies were given the opportunity to trade their 401(k) assets using an Internet service. The advantage of studying these trades is that because they occurred within a qualified pension plan, liquidity needs and tax-loss selling were not factors. All trades can be considered speculative. Their conclusions were consistent with overconfident trading; specifically, they found that trading frequency doubled and portfolio turnover increased by 50 percent.

Online Trading and Performance

Barber and Odean also examined the performance of the investors before and after going online. Before switching to the online trading service, these investors were successful. As illustrated in Figure 2.3, they earned nearly 18 percent per year before going online. This represents a return of 2.35 percent more than the stock market in general. However, after going online, these investors experienced reduced returns. They averaged annual returns of only 12 percent, underperforming the market by 3.5 percent.

The successful performance of these investors before going online might have fostered overconfidence due to the illusion of control (via the outcome sequence). This overconfidence might have caused them to choose an Internet trading service. Unfortunately, the Internet trading environment exacerbates the overconfidence problem, inducing excessive trading. Ultimately, investor returns are reduced.

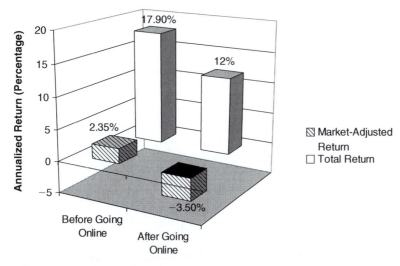

FIGURE 2.3   Annualized Market-Adjusted Return and Total Return of Investors Before and After Switching to an Online Trading System

Summary

People can be overconfident about their abilities, knowledge, and future prospects. Overconfidence leads to excessive trading, which lowers portfolio returns. Lower returns result from the commission costs associated with high levels of trading and the propensity to purchase stocks that underperform the stocks that are sold. Overconfidence also leads to greater risk taking due to underdiversification and a focus on investing in small companies with higher betas. Individual investors are most likely to get overconfident after experiencing high returns, like after a strong bull market. Finally, the trend of using online brokerage accounts is making investors more overconfident than ever before.

Questions

1. Would you expect investors to be more overconfident in the midst of a bull market or a bear market? Why?
2. How might an investor's portfolio have changed from 1995 to 2000 if the investor had become overconfident? Give examples of the numbers and types of stocks in the portfolio.
3. How does the Internet trick investors into believing they have wisdom?
4. How might using an online broker (versus a full-service broker) create an illusion of control?

Notes

1. Ola Svenson, "Are We All Less Risky and More Skillful Than Our Fellow Drivers?" *Acta Psychologica* 47(1981): 143–148.
2. Arnold C. Cooper, Carolyn Y. Woo, and William C. Dunkelberg, "Entrepreneurs' Perceived Chances for Success," *Journal of Business Venturing* 3(1988): 97–108.
3. E. J. Langer, "The Illusion of Control," *Journal of Personality and Social Psychology* 32(1975): 311–328.
4. Gilles Hilary and Lior Menzly, "Does Past Success Lead Analysts to Become Overconfident?" *Management Science* 52(2006): 489–500.
5. Brad Barber and Terrance Odean, "The Courage of Misguided Convictions," *Financial Analysts Journal* (November/December 1999): 41–55.
6. Sylvia Beyer and Edward Bowden, "Gender Differences in Self-Perceptions: Convergent Evidence from Three Measures of Accuracy and Bias," *Journal of Personality and Social Psychology* 59(1997): 960–970. See also Melvin Prince, "Women, Men, and Money Styles," *Journal of Economic Psychology* 14(1993): 175–182.
7. Brad Barber and Terrance Odean, "Boys Will Be Boys: Gender, Overconfidence, and Common Stock Investment," *Quarterly Journal of Economics* 116(2001): 261–292.
8. Brad Barber and Terrance Odean, "Trading Is Hazardous to Your Wealth: The Common Stock Investment Performance of Individual Investors," *Journal of Finance* 55(2000): 773–806.
9. Terrance Odean, "Do Investors Trade Too Much?" *American Economic Review* 89(1999): 1279–1298.
10. Markus Glaser and Martin Weber, "Overconfidence and Trading Volume," *Geneva Risk and Insurance Review* 32:1(2007): 1–36.
11. Meir Statman, Steven Thorley, and Keith Vorkink, "Investor Overconfidence and Trading Volume," *Review of Financial Studies* 19(2006): 1531–1565.
12. For a discussion and test of the illusion of knowledge, see Dane Peterson and Gordon Pitz, "Confidence, Uncertainty, and the Use of Information," *Journal of Experimental Psychology* 14(1988): 85–92.

13. W. Brooke Elliott, Frank D. Hodge, and Kevin E. Jackson, "The Association between Nonprofessional Investors' Information Choices and Their Portfolio Returns: The Importance of Investing Experience," *Contemporary Accounting Research* 25:2(2008): 473–498.

14. Ibid.

15. Michael Dewally, "Internet Investment Advice: Investing with a Rock of Salt," *Financial Analysts Journal* 59(July/August 2003): 65–77.

16. Robert Tumarkin and Robert F. Whitelaw, "News or Noise? Internet Postings and Stock Prices," *Financial Analysts Journal* (May/June 2001): 41–51.

17. Wen-I Chuang and Rauli Susmel, "Who Is the More Overconfident Trader? Individual vs. Institutional Investors," *Journal of Banking and Finance* 35(2011): 1626–1644.

18. Paul Presson and Victor Benassi, "Illusion of Control: A Meta-Analytic Review," *Journal of Social Behavior and Personality* 11(1996): 493–510.

19. Simon Gervais and Terrance Odean, "Learning to Be Overconfident," *Review of Financial Studies* 14(2001): 1–27. See also Kent Daniel, David Hirshleifer, and Avanidhar Subrahmanyam, "Overconfidence, Arbitrage, and Equilibrium Asset Pricing," *Journal of Finance* 56(2001): 921–965.

20. Brad Barber and Terrance Odean, "The Internet and the Investor," *Journal of Economic Perspectives* 15(2001): 41–54.

21. Brad Barber and Terrance Odean, "Online Investors: Do the Slow Die First?" *Review of Financial Studies* 15(2002): 455–487.

22. James Choi, David Laibson, and Andrew Metrick, "How Does the Internet Increase Trading? Evidence from Investor Behavior in 401(k) Plans," *Journal of Financial Economics* 64(2002): 397–421.

Pride and Regret

People avoid actions that create regret and seek actions that cause pride. Regret is the emotional pain that comes with realizing that a previous decision turned out to be a bad one. Pride is the emotional joy of realizing that a decision turned out well.

Consider the following example of the state lottery.[1] You have been selecting the same lottery ticket numbers every week for months. Not surprisingly, you have not won. A friend suggests a different set of numbers. Will you change your numbers?

Clearly, the likelihood of the old set of numbers winning is the same as the likelihood of the new set of numbers winning. This example has two possible sources of regret. Regret will result if you stick with the old numbers and the new numbers win. This is called the regret of omission (not acting). Regret also will result if you switch to the new numbers and the old numbers win. The regret of an action you took is the regret of commission. In which case would the pain of regret be stronger? The stronger regret would most likely result from switching to the new numbers because you have invested a lot of emotional capital in the old numbers—after all, you have been selecting them for months. Generally, a regret of commission is more painful than a regret of omission. Investors often regret the actions they take, but seldom regret the ones they do not.

DISPOSITION EFFECT

Avoiding regret and seeking pride affects people's behavior, but how does it affect investment decisions? Two financial economists, Hersh Shefrin and Meir Statman, studied this psychological behavior of investors making decisions.[2]

They showed that fearing regret and seeking pride causes investors to be predisposed to selling winners too early and riding losers too long. They call this the *disposition effect*.

Consider the situation in which you wish to invest in a particular stock. However, you have no cash and must sell another stock in order to have the cash for the new purchase. You can sell either of two stocks you hold. Stock A has earned a 20 percent return since you purchased it, whereas stock B has lost 20 percent. Which stock do you sell? Selling stock A validates your good decision to purchase it in the first place. It would make you feel proud to lock in your profit. Selling stock B at a loss means realizing that your decision to purchase it was bad. You would feel the pain of regret. The disposition effect predicts that you will sell the winner, stock A. Selling stock A triggers the feeling of pride and allows you to avoid regret.

DISPOSITION EFFECT AND WEALTH

Why is it a problem that investors may sell their winners more frequently than their losers? One reason relates to the U.S. tax code. The taxation of capital gains causes the selling of losers to be a wealth-maximizing strategy. Selling a winner leads to the realization of a capital gain and hence payment of taxes. Those taxes reduce your profit. On the other hand, selling the losers gives you a chance to reduce your taxes, thus decreasing the amount of the loss. Reconsider the previously mentioned example and assume that capital gains are taxed at the rate of 15 percent (Table 3.1). If your positions in stocks A and B are each valued at $1,000, then the original purchase price of stock A must have been $833, and the purchase price of stock B must have been $1,250.

If you sell stock A, you receive $1,000 but you pay taxes of $26.55, so your net proceeds are $973.45. Alternatively, you could sell stock B and receive $1,000 plus gain a tax credit of $37.50 to be used against other capital gains, so your net proceeds are $1,037.50. If the tax rate is higher than 15 percent (as in the case of gains realized within one year of the stock purchase), then the advantage of selling the loser is even greater. Interestingly, the disposition effect predicts the selling of winners, even though selling the losers is a wealth-maximizing strategy.

TABLE 3.1   Capital Gains and Taxation

Sell	Stock A (in $)	Stock B (in $)
Sale Proceeds	1,000	1,000
Tax Basis	833	1,250
Taxable Gain (Loss)	177	(250)
Tax (Credit) at 15%	26.55	(37.50)
After-Tax Proceeds	973.45	1,037.50

TESTS OF AVOIDING REGRET AND SEEKING PRIDE

Do investors behave in a rational manner by predominantly selling losers, or are investors affected by their psychology and have a tendency to sell their winners? Several studies provide evidence that investors behave in a manner more consistent with the disposition effect (selling winners). These studies generally fall into two categories: studies that examine the stock market and those that examine investor trades.

For example, Ferris et al.[3] examined the trading volume of stocks following price changes. If investors trade to maximize wealth, then they should sell stocks with price declines and capture the tax benefits. In addition, they should refrain from selling stocks with price gains to avoid paying taxes. Therefore, the volume of trades should be high for stocks with losses and low for stocks with gains. Alternatively, investors may opt to avoid regret and seek pride. In this case, it would be expected that investors will hold their losers and sell their winners. Therefore, high volume in the stocks with gains and low volume in the stocks with declines is consistent with the disposition effect.

Ferris et al. used a methodology that determined the normal level of volume expected for each stock. They reported results that could be interpreted as a form of abnormal volume; that is, a negative abnormal volume indicates less trading than normal, whereas a positive abnormal volume indicates more trading than normal. Using the 30 smallest stocks on the New York Stock Exchange (NYSE) and the American Stock Exchange from December 1981 to January 1985, they grouped each stock into categories based on the percentage gain or loss at each point in time. The results are presented in Figure 3.1.

Note that the stocks with losses of more than 22.5 percent are grouped in the left column. The loss diminishes in each column to the right until the middle of the graph, where stocks had small losses or gains. Stocks in the far-right column had a gain of more than 22.5 percent. In general, stocks with gains had positive abnormal volume, whereas stocks with declines had negative abnormal volume. Higher volume in stocks with gains and lower volume in stocks with declines is consistent with the disposition effect.

This analysis was performed separately for stock volume in December and the rest of the year because people are more aware of the benefits of

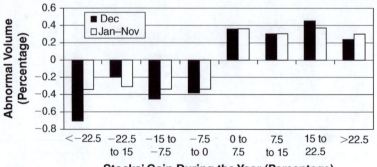

FIGURE 3.1 Volume of Stocks After Losses and Gains

selling losers and gaining tax advantages in December. Therefore, it would seem that investors might be more likely to enact a wealth-maximizing strategy in December versus the other months. However, Figure 3.1 shows that investors avoid regret and seek pride as much in December as during the rest of the year.

Other studies have analyzed the actual trades and portfolios of individual investors. In an older study using trades from a national brokerage house from 1964 to 1970, Schlarbaum et al. examined 75,000 round-trip trades.[4] A round-trip trade is a stock purchase followed later by the sale of the stock.

They examined the length of time the stock was held and the return that was received. Are investors quick to close out a position when it has taken a loss or when it has had a gain? Consider the behavior implied by the disposition effect. If you buy a stock that goes up quickly, you will be more inclined to sell it quickly. If you buy a stock that goes down or remains level, you are more inclined to hold while waiting for it to go up. Therefore, stocks held for a short time tend to be winners, and stocks held longer are likely to be less successful. Figure 3.2 shows the average annualized return for a position held for less than 1 month, 1 to 6 months, 6 to 12 months, and more than one year. The figure indicates that investors are quick to realize their gains. The average annualized return for stocks purchased then sold within 1 month was 45 percent. The returns for stocks held 1 to 6 months, 6 to 12 months, and more than one year were 7.8 percent, 5.1 percent, and 4.5 percent, respectively. It appears that investors are quick to sell winners.

Using a more recent sample, Terrance Odean studied the trades of 10,000 trading accounts from a nationwide discount brokerage from 1987 to 1993.[5] At each sell trade, Odean calculated the amount of gains and losses the investor had on paper in his or her portfolio. If the investor sold a winner, then Odean calculated the gain on the stock and divided the value by the total paper gains available to the investor. The result is the proportion of total gains that the investor realized with the sell trade. If the stock sold was a loser, then the proportion of total losses realized was computed.

Odean found that when investors sell winners, the sale represents 23 percent of the total gains of the investors' portfolio. Alternatively, when a loser is

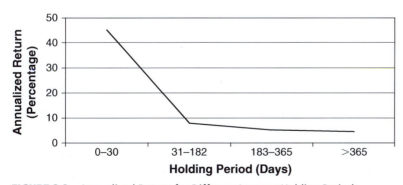

FIGURE 3.2   Annualized Return for Different Investor Holding Periods

sold, it represents only 15.5 percent of the unrealized losses in the portfolio. On average, investors are 50 percent more likely to sell a winner than a loser.

However, the propensity to sell a stock seems to be greater for stocks with higher profits. In other words, investors can achieve more pride when the profit realized is larger. But this does not appear to be the case for selling losers.[6] Investors are reluctant to sell a loser. That reluctance is no greater for big losers than it is for small losers. Regret seems to be measured as a loss. However, the magnitude of the loss does not seem to play much of a role in avoiding the regret.

International Tests of the Disposition Effect

Researchers have found the disposition effect to be pervasive. Investors in Finland, Israel, and China exhibit the behavior. Mark Grinblatt and Matti Keloharju studied all investor trades in Finland during 1995 and 1996.[7] They found that a large positive return the previous week significantly increased an investor's propensity to sell the stock. On the other hand, a large decrease in price significantly increased the probability that the investor will hold the stock. They also found that the more recently the stock gains or losses occurred (last week versus last month), the stronger the propensity was to sell winners and hold losers. Interestingly, they also find that financial institutions succumb to the disposition effect nearly as much as individual investors do, though institutions are more likely to sell their losers than other investors. Among investors in Israel, Zur Shapira and Itzhak Venezia found that individual investors held on to winner stocks for an average of 20 days and loser stocks for 43 days.[8] Investors hold losers twice as long as winners! Chinese investors also realize more gains than losses and hold losers 10 days longer than winners.[9]

Disposition Outside the Stock Market

Most of the evidence for the disposition effect has been found in the various stock markets around the world. How much of an impact does avoiding regret and seeking pride have in other markets? Several studies have found that futures traders (trading in agricultural, bond, currency, and stock index futures contracts) hold on to losses significantly longer than gains, and traders who hold on to positions longer make less profit.[10] Corporate managers with employee stock options exhibit a disposition effect in their willingness to exercise those options.[11] In the real estate market, homeowners are reluctant to sell their homes below their original purchase price.[12]

One area in which investors do not seem to exhibit the disposition effect is in mutual fund share ownership. Several studies found that investors are more willing to sell shares in a losing mutual fund and reluctant to sell winner funds.[13] This behavior is the opposite of loss aversion and the disposition effect. One explanation may be that investors are not as reluctant to realize a loss if they can blame someone else for the problem. If an investor can blame the portfolio manager or a financial advisor, then the investor feels less regret.

SELLING WINNERS TOO SOON AND
HOLDING LOSERS TOO LONG

The disposition effect not only predicts the selling of winners but also suggests that the winners are sold too soon and the losers are held too long. What does selling too soon or holding too long imply for investors? Selling winners too soon suggests that those stocks will continue to perform well after they are sold. Holding losers too long suggests that those stocks with price declines will continue to perform poorly.

When an investor sold a winning stock, Odean found that the stock generally beat the market during the next year by an average of 2.35 percent.[14] During this same year, the loser stocks that the investors kept generally underperformed the market by –1.06 percent. Investors tend to sell the stock that ends up providing a high return and keep the stock that provides a low return.

Note that the fear of regret and the seeking of pride hurt investors' wealth in two ways. First, investors are paying more in taxes because of the disposition to sell winners instead of losers. Second, investors earn a lower return on their portfolio because they sell the winners too early and hold poorly performing stocks that continue to perform poorly.

Martin Weber and Colin Camerer designed a stock trading experiment for their students.[15] They created six "stocks" for trading and showed the students the last three price points of each stock. They designed the experiment so that the stock prices are likely to trend; that is, stocks with gains will likely continue to gain, whereas stocks with declines will likely continue to decline. The students are shown the potential prices for each stock in the future. Because of this experimental design, stocks with losses should be sold and stocks with gains should be held (the opposite of the disposition effect). Contrary to the wealth-maximizing strategy, the student subjects sold fewer shares when the price was below the purchase price than when the price was above, thus exhibiting the disposition effect.

DISPOSITION EFFECT AND NEWS

One study investigated all the trades of individual investors in 144 NYSE firms during the period of November 1990 through January 1991.[16] Specifically, the study investigated how investors reacted to news about the firms and news about the economy. News about a company primarily affects the price of the company's stock, whereas economic news affects all firms. Good news about a firm that increases the firm's stock price induces investors to sell (selling winners). Bad news about a firm does not induce investors to sell (holding losers). This is consistent with avoiding regret and seeking pride.

However, news about the economy does not induce investor trading. Although good economic news increases stock prices and bad economic news lowers stock prices, this does not cause individual investors to sell. In fact, investors are less likely than usual to sell winners after good economic news. These results are not consistent with the disposition effect.

This illustrates an interesting characteristic of regret. When taking a stock loss, investors feel stronger regret if the loss can be tied to their own decisions.

However, if investors can attribute the loss to reasons that are out of their control, then the feeling of regret is weaker.[17] For example, if the stock you hold declines in price when the stock market itself is advancing, then you have made a bad choice, and regret is strong. However, if the stock you hold declines in price during a general market decline, then this is essentially out of your control, so the feeling of regret is weak.

Investor actions are consistent with the disposition effect for company news because the feeling of regret is strong. In the case of economic news, investors have a weaker feeling of regret because the outcome is considered beyond their control. This leads to actions that are not consistent with the predictions of the disposition effect.

REFERENCE POINTS

The pleasure of achieving gains and the pain of losses is a powerful motivator of human behavior. However, it might be difficult to determine whether some investment transactions are considered a profit or a loss. For example, Bob purchases a stock for $50 per share. At the end of the year, the stock is trading for $100. Also at end of the year, Bob reexamines his investment positions in order to record and determine his net worth and monitor the progress he has made toward his financial goals. Six months later, Bob sells the stock for $75 per share. He has made a profit of $25 per share. However, the profit is $25 per share lower than if he had sold at the end of the year. Clearly, he made a $25-per-share profit. However, does Bob feel like he made a profit, or does he feel like he lost money?

This issue deals with a *reference point*. A reference point is the stock price that we compare with the current stock price. The current stock price is $75. Is the reference point the purchase price of $50 or the end-of-year price of $100? The brain's choice of a reference point is important because it determines whether we feel the pleasure of obtaining a profit or the pain of a loss.

An interesting example of whether reference points matter is the case of the initial public offering (IPO). Markku Kaustia examined the volume in IPO trading between stocks that trade above their offer price versus those that trade below their offer price.[18] For a stock to trade, there must be someone who is willing to sell. The disposition effect suggests that investors are more willing to sell when the stock is a winner and are reluctant to sell when it is a loser. Thus, volume should be higher for IPOs trading above their offer price because they are winners when disposition impacts these investors. He finds that volume is lower for IPOs selling below their offer price as investors are reluctant to sell the newly purchased stock at a loss. Volume is higher for IPOs trading above the offer price. Those investors seem to be more willing to realize a quick profit by selling. In fact, the greater the gain in the stock, the higher the ensuing trading volume.

The early investigations into the psychology of investors assumed that the purchase price was the reference point. This makes IPOs a great test because the purchase price is known for most of the investors selling the stock on the first day. However, investors monitor and remember their investment performance over the period of a year. If the purchase was made long ago, then investors tend to use a more recently determined reference point.

What recent stock price is used as a reference? When thinking about the stock market in general, investors use indexes to gain the performance of stocks. One of the most widely reported indices is, of course, the Dow Jones Industrial Average. Investors tend to use the Dow's all time high and the 52-week high as important reference points.[19]

Regarding individual stocks, an interesting investigation of the exercising of stock options illustrates a reference point.[20] Stock options have a premium value in addition to the fundamental value derived from the difference between the option's strike price and the underlying stock price. In other words, even out-of-the-money options have a positive value. The premium declines to zero on the option's expiration date. Because of this premium, it is almost never optimal to exercise an option before the expiration date. If a trader wants to lock in a profit, then selling the option results in more value than exercising it and receiving the stock shares. Yet, Allen Poteshman and Vitaly Serbin found a large number of early option exercises of exchange-traded stock options, which often occurred months before the expiration date. What would motivate these investors to choose this irrational behavior?

They found that a trigger occurs when the underlying stock price reaches or exceeds its 52-week high. This suggests that the recent highest price is an important reference point for investors. In fact, it is such a strong focus for the option traders that when the stock price climbs above this reference, traders rush to lock in profits. Some of them even irrationally exercise the options. It appears that this problem can be avoided though. Customers of discount brokers execute these irrational trades more than customers of full-service brokers. The professional traders did not make this mistake.

REFERENCE POINT ADAPTATION

In the opening illustration or in this section, would Bob consider the purchase price of $50 to be his reference point, or the recent year-end price of $100, or something else? In other words, do investors adapt their reference points over time?

Yes, it appears that investors would adapt their reference point over time. How they adapt it is similar to the disposition effect! Consider the shape of prospect theory's utility function shown in Chapter 1. After Bob's stock has earned a $50 profit, he feels good about it. Investors tend to sell the stock and lock-in that happiness. It seems that investors can lock-in some of that happiness by holding onto the stocks and simply shifting their reference point. A research paper that examines this possibility surveys people and asks them about how much prices must go up a second time in order to feel as good as the first profit.[21] By comparing the answers to the prospect theory utility function, the authors can determine how much the investors have moved the reference point after the initial stock price increase. A similar analysis is done for stock declines and losses.

The results of the study are consistent with prospect theory. Because of the shape of the utility function, investors would be happier if they experienced two separate $50 profits rather than one $100 profit. This is one way to explain the disposition effect. Investors sell their winners quickly in order to feel the happiness and set themselves up for another profit in another trade. It now appears that investors can get the same effect by changing the reference point after the profit and then considering the holding of the stock to be a new trade. Also consider the sadness we feel after a loss. Investors try to minimize the regret by holding the loser and not locking-in the negative emotion. How would that impact reference point adaptation? Investors would not want to implicitly lock-in the sadness by shifting the reference point like they do for winners. This is exactly what the research shows. People increase their reference points on stocks they hold more for winners than for losers.

Returning to the illustration with Bob, he probably feels like he lost money because he would have moved his reference point to $100 when he recorded that price in his end-of-year evaluation.

CAN THE DISPOSITION EFFECT IMPACT THE MARKET?

Professors Vijay Singal and Zhaojin Xu examined the portfolios and trading of mutual funds.[22] They find that 30 percent of mutual funds exhibit the disposition effect. These disposition funds underperform the other funds by 4 to 6 percent per year and are more likely to be closed. Can the presence of a large group of investors suffering from the disposition effect impact market prices? Andrea Frazzini provided evidence that it does.[23] Consider a stock that has risen in price and has many investors who hold capital gains in it. If this firm announces good news (like a great earnings report), the selling of this winner will temporarily depress the stock price from fully rising to its deserved new level. From this lower price base, subsequent returns will be higher. This price pattern is known as an "underreaction" to news and a postannouncement price drift. Frazzini showed that the postannouncement drift occurs primarily in winner stocks where investors have unrealized capital gains and loser stocks with unrealized capital losses.

Frazzini first analyzed mutual fund holding data and found that they also displayed the disposition effect. In fact, the managers of funds that performed the worst were the most reluctant to close their losing positions. To estimate the amount of unrealized capital gains (or losses) in each stock, an average cost basis of the mutual funds was computed. This basis was used as the reference point in comparison to current prices. Many investors consider stocks with current prices higher than the reference point as winner stocks with unrealized capital gains. The largest positive postannouncement drift occurs for stocks with good news and large unrealized capital gains. The largest negative drift occurs for stocks with bad news and large unrealized capital losses. This pattern is consistent with disposition investors quickly selling winners, preventing the stock price from initially rising to its new level. Disposition investors are also reluctant to sell losers, thus underreacting to negative news about these firms.

DISPOSITION AND INVESTOR SOPHISTICATION

Do loss aversion and the disposition effect impact all investors? Can we learn to avoid it? It is hoped that once we learn about a behavioral bias, we become more investment savvy and can avoid that problem. Indeed, it appears that more-sophisticated investors exhibit lower levels of loss aversion and the disposition effect than less-sophisticated investors. For example, investors with higher incomes exhibit lower disposition than those with lower incomes. There is lower disposition for investors with a professional occupation versus a nonprofessional job.[24]

Do professional investors exhibit the disposition effect? In general, the answer is yes. As described earlier, professional futures traders, mutual fund managers, and other money managers tend to realize gains at a faster rate than realizing losses. Is it because losing positions are more likely to do better in the future than profitable positions, or do the managers have a sunk emotional cost associated with these positions? Li Jin and Anna Scherbina seem to think it is the latter. They studied the changes made in mutual fund portfolios when a new portfolio manager takes over.[25] They find that the new manager, who has no regret aversion to these inherited positions, sells these underperforming positions more than other mutual funds and more than the highly performing positions.

BUYING BACK STOCK PREVIOUSLY SOLD

One investor behavior that seems odd from the perspective of traditional finance is the fact that investors tend to sell a stock and then repurchase it again later. In fact, investors often buy and sell the same stock many times. Regret plays a role in whether an investor will repurchase a stock. Investors who are happy with the outcome of a completed trade want to relive that happiness and do so by repurchasing the same stock. An unhappy feeling with a trade is not to be relived; it is to be avoided. So, stocks that bring back regret are not repurchased.

Terrance Odean teamed up with Brad Barber and Michal Ann Strahilevitz to explain this behavior.[26] They illustrate how emotion is induced after the sale of a stock. As Figure 3.3 shows, there are two factors that influence the emotion created from a stock sale—the profit of the trade and the movement of the price after the sale. When investors sell a stock at a loss, the negative emotion of regret is painful enough so that there is no desire to repurchase the stock.

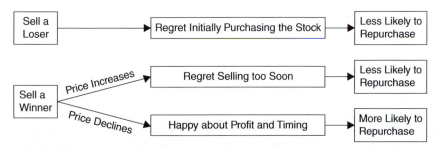

FIGURE 3.3 The Dynamics of Repurchasing a Stock Previously Sold

Once burned, twice shy. You might think that selling a winner creates a positive emotion. While that is true, the emotion is short lived and is impacted by how the stock's price changes after the sale. If the price continues to go up, then the happiness starts to change to regret as the investor wishes he had not sold it so soon. Between the initial happiness and the later regret, it is the negative emotion that lasts. So no repurchase occurs. However, when a winner stock is sold and the price subsequently falls, the investor feels doubly happy due to the profit and the great timing of the sale. Investors are more likely to repurchase this stock.

Studying actual trades of investors during 1991 to 1999, the authors find that the frequency of repurchasing a stock previously sold is consistent with the emotion experienced in the previous trade. They find that investors repurchase a stock three times more frequently if it was a winner and the price falls after the sale compared to if it was a loser. Indeed, once burned, twice shy.

Summary

People act (or fail to act) to avoid regret and seek pride, which causes investors to sell their winners too soon and hold their losers too long—the disposition effect. This behavior hurts investor wealth in two ways. First, investors pay more capital gains taxes because they sell winners. Second, investors earn a lower return because the winners they sell no longer continue to perform well, while the losers they still hold continue to perform poorly. The disposition effect can be seen in investor trades, market volume, and other markets like real estate and derivatives trading. A common rule of thumb to avoid letting the disposition effect impact you is to "cut your losses and let your profits run."

Experiencing regret also causes investors to be less likely to repurchase the same loser stock later. However, investors do like to relive the good experience of selling a winner and watching a subsequent decline in the stock's price.

Questions

1. Consider an investor's statement: "If the stock price would only get back up to what I paid for it, I'd sell it!" Describe how the biases in this chapter are influencing the investor's decision.
2. How would the number of stocks held in the portfolio impact the disposition effect?
3. How can succumbing to the disposition effect harm wealth?
4. How can the disposition effect impact market prices?
5. Investors frequently repurchase a stock they previously owned and sold. Explain which stocks are they more likely to repurchase.

Notes

1. This example is adapted from Roger G. Clarke, Stock Krase, and Meir Statman, "Tracking Errors, Regret, and Tactical Asset Allocation," *Journal of Portfolio Management* 20(1994): 16–24.

2. Hersh Shefrin and Meir Statman, "The Disposition to Sell Winners Too Early and Ride Losers Too Long: Theory and Evidence," *Journal of Finance* 40(1985): 777–790.

3. Stephen P. Ferris, Robert A. Haugen, and Anil K. Makhija, "Predicting Contemporary Volume with Historic Volume at Differential Price Levels: Evidence Supporting the Disposition Effect," *Journal of Finance* 43(1987): 677–697.

4. Gary G. Schlarbaum, Wilbur G. Lewellen, and Ronald C. Lease, "Realized Returns on Common Stock Investments: The Experience of Individual Investors," *Journal of Business* 51(1978): 299–325.

5. Terrance Odean, "Are Investors Reluctant to Realize Their Losses?" *Journal of Finance* 53(1998): 1775–1798.

6. See Markku Kaustia, "Prospect Theory and the Disposition Effect," *Journal of Financial and Quantitative Analysis*, 45(2010): 791–812.

7. Mark Grinblatt and Matti Keloharju, "What Makes Investors Trade?" *Journal of Finance* 56(2001): 589–616.

8. Zur Shapira and Itzhak Venezia, "Patterns of Behavior of Professionally Managed and Independent Investors," *Journal of Banking and Finance* 25(2001): 1573–1587.

9. Gongmeng Chen, Kenneth Kim, John Nofsinger, and Oliver Rui, "Trading Performance, Disposition Effect, Overconfidence, Representativeness Bias, and Experience of Emerging Market Investors," *Journal of Behavioral Decision Making* 20(2007): 425–451.

10. See Hyuk Choe and Yunsung Eom, "The Disposition Effect and Investment Performance in the Future Market," *Journal of Futures Markets* 29(2009): 496–522; Joshua Coval and Tyler Shumway, "Do Behavioral Biases Affect Prices?" *Journal of Finance* 60(2005): 1–34; and Peter Locke and Steven Mann, "Professional Trader Discipline and Trade Disposition," *Journal of Financial Economics* 76(2005): 401–444.

11. Chip Heath, Steven Huddart, and Mark Lang, "Psychological Factors and Stock Option Exercise," *Quarterly Journal of Economics* 114(1999): 601–627.

12. David Genesove and Christopher Mayer, "Loss Aversion and Seller Behavior: Evidence from the Housing Market," *Quarterly Journal of Economics* 116(2001): 1233–1260.

13. See Laurent Calvet, John Campbell, and Paolo Sodini, "Fight or Flight? Portfolio Rebalancing by Individual Investors," *Quarterly Journal of Economics* 124(2009): 301–348 and Xoran Ivkovic and Scott Weisbenner, "Individual Investor Mutual Fund Flows," *Journal of Financial Economics* 92(2009): 223–237.

14. Actually, Odean calculates an abnormal return that is based not on the market but rather on matching firms.

15. Martin Weber and Colin F. Camerer, "The Disposition Effect in Securities Trading: An Experimental Analysis," *Journal of Economic Behavior and Organization* 33(1998): 167–184.

16. John R. Nofsinger, "The Impact of Public Information on Investors," *Journal of Banking and Finance* 25(2001): 1339–1366.

17. This discussion is adapted from Roger G. Clarke, Stock Krase, and Meir Statman, "Tracking Errors, Regret, and Tactical Asset Allocation," *Journal of Portfolio Management* 20(1994): 19.

18. Markku Kaustia, "Market-wide Impact of the Disposition Effect: Evidence from IPO Trading Volume," *Journal of Financial Markets* 7(2004): 207–235.

19. See Jun Li and Jianfeng Yu, "Investor Attention, Psychological Anchors, and Stock Return Predictability," *Journal of Financial Economics* 104(2012): 401–419.

20. See Allen Poteshman and Vitaly Serbin, "Clearly Irrational Financial Market Behavior: Evidence from the Early Exercise of Exchange Traded Stock Options," *Journal of Finance* 58(2003): 37–70.

21. Hal R. Arkes, David A. Hirshleifer, Danling Jiang, and Sonya S. Lim, "Reference Point Adaptation: Tests in the Domain of Security Trading," *Organization Behavior and Human Decision Processes* 105(2008): 67–81.

22. Vijay Singal and Zhaojin Xu, "Selling Winners, Holding Losers: Effect on Fund Flows and Survival of Disposition-prone Mutual Funds," *Journal of Banking and Finance* 35(2011): 2704–2718.

23. Andrea Frazzini, "The Disposition Effect and Underreaction to News," *Journal of Finance* 61(2006): 2017–2046.

24. See Ravi Dhar and Ning Zhu, "Up Close and Personal: Investor Sophistication and the Disposition Effect," *Management Science* 52(2006): 726–740.

25. Li Jin and Anna Scherbina, "Inheriting Losers," *Review of Financial Studies* 24(2011), 786–820.

26. Michal Ann Strahilevitz, Terrance Odean, and Brad M. Barber, "Once Burned, Twice Shy: How Naïve Learning, Counterfactuals, and Regret Affect the Repurchase of Stocks Previously Sold," *Journal of Marking Research* 48(2011), S102–S120.

4

Risk Perceptions

A person who has not made peace with his losses is likely to accept gambles that would be unacceptable to him otherwise.

KAHNEMAN AND TVERSKY[1]

Consider this wager on a coin toss: Heads you win $20, tails you lose $20. Would you take this gamble? By the way, you won $100 earlier. Now would you take this gamble? Did your answer change after finding out that you had won earlier? What if you had lost $20 earlier? Would this make the gamble look any different to you?

Many people will take the gamble in one situation but not in another. The odds of winning the $20 do not change in the different scenarios, so the expected value of the gamble remains the same. Neither the risk nor the reward of the gamble changes between situations; therefore, people's reaction to risk must change.

People's perception of risk does appear to vary. One important factor in evaluating a current risky decision is a past outcome. In short, people are willing to take more risk after earning gains and less risk after sustaining losses. To illustrate this behavior, Richard Thaler and Eric Johnson asked 95 undergraduate economics students to take a series of two-step gambles using real money.[2] In the first step, money was either given to or taken from the student. In the second step, the student was asked whether he or she wished to take the gamble presented. Their findings suggest a "house-money effect," a risk-aversion (or snakebite) effect, and a "trying-to-break-even effect," which are discussed in the following sections.

HOUSE-MONEY EFFECT

After people have experienced a gain or profit, they are willing to take more risk. Gamblers refer to this feeling as playing with the house's money. After winning a big sum, amateur gamblers do not fully consider the new money as their own. Are you willing to take more risk with your opponent's money or your own money? Because gamblers don't fully integrate their winnings with their own money, they act like they are betting with the casino's money.

You have just won $15. Now you are faced with the opportunity to bet $4.50 on a coin toss. Do you place the bet? Seventy-seven percent of the economics students placed the bet. After just receiving their windfall of $15, most students were willing to take the risk. On the other hand, when students were asked to place a bet on a coin toss without receiving the $15, only 41 percent chose the gamble. Students are more willing to take a financial risk after a windfall profit even when not ordinarily inclined to take such a risk.

SNAKEBITE (OR RISK AVERSION)

After experiencing a financial loss, people become less willing to take a risk. When faced with a gamble after already losing money, people generally choose to decline the gamble. Students who initially lost $7.50 were then asked to wager $2.25 on the flip of a coin. This time, the majority (60 percent) declined the gamble. After losing the initial money, the students might have felt "snakebit."

Snakes do not often bite people, but when they do, people become more cautious. Likewise, after having been unlucky enough to lose money, people often feel they will continue to be unlucky; therefore, they avoid risk.

TRYING TO BREAK EVEN

Losers do not always avoid risk. People often jump at the chance to make up their losses. After having lost some money, a majority of the students accepted a "double-or-nothing" toss of the coin. In fact, a majority of the students were willing to accept a double-or-nothing toss of the coin even when they were told the coin was not "fair"; that is, students were willing to take a risk, even though they knew they had less than a 50 percent chance of winning. The need for breaking even appears to be stronger than the snakebite effect.

Another example of this break-even effect can be seen at the racetrack. After a day of betting on horses and losing money, gamblers are more likely to bet on long shots.[3] Odds of 15 to 1 mean that a $2 bet would win $30 if the horse wins. Of course, horses with odds of 15 to 1 are unlikely to win. The proportion of money bet on long shots is greater toward the end of the race day than at the beginning. It appears that gamblers are less likely to take this risk early in the day. However, those gamblers who have won money (house-money effect) or lost money (break-even effect) during the day are more likely to take this kind of risk. Winners take this risk because they feel as though they are playing with the house's money. Losers like the opportunity to break even without risking too much more. People without significant gains or losses prefer not to take the risk.

The willingness to increase the level of risk taken is periodically demonstrated in *Deal or No Deal*, a very popular TV show worldwide. In the show, a contestant picks one briefcase for himself or herself with an unknown amount of money in it. The contestant then picks 6 of the remaining 25 to be opened and removed from the game. In the U.S. version of the show, the briefcases have a known distribution of money ranging from $0.01 to $1,000,000. Removing the 6 briefcases leaves 20 and a new distribution of money left to win. The contestant is then given an offer of a specific amount of money to end the game. Should he take the sure thing, or gamble and keep playing? Consider that the expected value of the gamble might be $50,000 and the offer is $30,000. Note that this offer is less than (60 percent of) the expected value of the gamble. Highly risk-averse contestants may take the offer—less risk-averse people will continue to play and pick more briefcases to open. Picking high-value (low-value) briefcases will lower (raise) the next offer.

An analysis of *Deal or No Deal* shows that the level of risk aversion shown by the contestants depends on the earlier outcomes experienced.[4] Specifically, when a contestant is unlucky in selecting briefcases with high-value monetary amounts to open, the next offer will then be lower than the previous one. Since the contestant is anchored on the previous offer, the new one feels like a "loss" of money. When this occurs, contestants rarely take the new offer and instead gamble in order to catch up or get even. This appears to be true even when an extremely good offer is given. Refer back to the expected gamble of $50,000 and regard it as the last two briefcases that happen to hold $100,000 and $0.01. What if the sure-thing offer was for $60,000? All else equal, nearly everyone would take the certain $60,000 over this risky gamble with a lower expected payoff. But all else is not equal if the last offer was for a larger amount, say, $90,000. The desire to "break even" appears to cause contestants to seek risky gambles. They seem to seek these risky gambles only after seeing the expected payoff (and thus the following offer) tumble.

Lastly, consider the professional, full-time proprietary traders in the treasury bond futures contract at the Chicago Board of Trade. These traders take risky positions during the day and provide market-making services to earn a profit. All positions are usually closed out by the end of the day. With a single-day focus on profits, what do these traders do in the afternoon when they have lost money in the morning? Joshua Coval and Tyler Shumway examined the trades of 426 such traders in 1998.[5] They found that after losing money in the morning, the traders are more likely to increase their level of risk in the afternoon in an attempt to make back the losses. In addition, these traders are more likely to trade with other proprietary traders (instead of orders coming into the market from investors). These trades turn out to be, on average, losing trades. This illustrates the change in behavior that an investor might exhibit after experiencing a loss.

EFFECT ON INVESTORS

The house-money effect predicts that investors are more likely to purchase risky stocks after closing out a successful position. In other words, after locking in a gain by selling stock at a profit, investors are more likely to buy higher-risk stocks. Massimo Massa and Andrei Simonov studied households in Sweden with data on both real estate and stock holdings.[6] They find that increases in capital gains one year leads to a higher amount of risk-taking in the following year, which is consistent with the house-money effect. Losses lead to decreased risk-taking—a snakebite reaction. Their findings hold for people in different wealth classes and for both real estate and stock market gains.

The snakebite effect can affect investors in other ways too. New or conservative investors might decide to "give the stock market a try." Adding some stocks to a portfolio gives the long-term investor better diversification and higher expected returns. However, if those stocks quickly decline in price, the first-time stock investor might feel snakebit. Consider a young investor who began by buying shares of a biotechnology company at $30 per share. Three days later, the stock price declined to $28, and the investor panicked and sold the stock. Later the stock went up to $75, but he or she is "afraid to get back in the market."[7]

ENDOWMENT (OR STATUS QUO BIAS) EFFECTS

People often demand much more to sell an object than they would be willing to pay to buy it. This is known as the endowment effect.[8] A closely related behavior is a person's tendency to keep what he or she has been given instead of exchanging it, known as status quo bias.[9]

Economists have examined the endowment effect by conducting experiments using their students. A common experiment is to give an object such as a university coffee mug to half the students in class. An ensuing market is created so that those students with mugs who do not want them can sell them to students who want the mugs but do not have them. Traditional economic theory predicts that a market-clearing price will develop such that half the mugs will exchange hands. That is, half the students who were given mugs will sell them to half the students who did not receive a mug. However, in repeated experiments, students endowed with a mug typically demand twice the price that students without a mug are willing to pay. As a consequence, few mugs are actually traded. This finding also occurs in experiments using different objects and using a repeating game, where students gain experience trading in this type of market.[10]

What creates this endowment effect? Do people overestimate the value of the objects they own, or does parting with them cause too much pain? Consider the following experiment.[11] Students were asked to rank the attractiveness of six prizes. A less-attractive prize, a pen, was given to half the students in the class. The other half of the class had a choice between the pen and two chocolate bars. Only 24 percent of the students picked the pen. The students who were originally given the pen were then given the opportunity to switch to the chocolate bars if they wanted. Even though most students ranked the chocolate higher than the pen as a prize, 56 percent of the students endowed with the pen elected not to switch. It does not appear that people overestimate the appeal of the object they own. Rather, they are more affected by the pain associated with giving up the object.

The endowment is also prevalent in people who routinely take part in real trading markets. For example, John List conducted trading experiments with collectible Cal Ripken and Nolan Ryan baseball memorabilia with customers and dealers at a sports card show.[12] He also conducted a similar experiment at the collector pin market at the Epcot Center. These participants were presumably familiar with trading. Yet, after receiving one collectible, few were willing to trade it for the other collectible of equal value. List found that the more-experienced dealers seemed to suffer less from the endowment effect.

Endowment and Investors

How can endowment or status quo bias affect investors? People have a tendency to hold the investments they already have. For example, William Samuelson and Richard Zeckhauser asked students to imagine that they just inherited a large sum of money. They could invest the money in different portfolios. Their choices were a moderate-risk company, a high-risk company, treasury bills, or municipal bonds.[13]

Many versions of this question were asked. In some versions, the subjects were told that the inheritance was already invested in a high-risk company. In other versions, the inheritance came in the form of the other investment options. Interestingly, the form of the investment at the time of endowment heavily influenced the portfolio choices made by the student subjects. The high-risk company choice was more popular when the inheritance was already invested in the high-risk company. The same was true for the treasury bill. Clearly, the expected risk and return of portfolios dominated by treasury bills and high-risk companies are very different; yet, subjects were more influenced by the status quo than by their own risk-and-return objectives. Financial advisors tell me that their clients are often willing to put a $100,000 windfall from a year-end bonus in the stock market but want to put a $100,000 windfall from an inheritance into a certificate of deposit. The clients say, "I can't take risk with that money; my parents worked very hard for it!"

The status quo bias increased as the number of investment options increased. That is, the more complicated the decision to be made, the more likely the subject was to choose to do nothing. In the real world, investors face the choice of investing in tens of thousands of company stocks, bonds, and mutual funds. All these choices may overwhelm some investors. As a result, they often choose to avoid making a change. This can be a particular problem when the investments have lost money. Selling a loser would trigger regret (Chapter 3) and the pain of losing the endowment.

PERCEPTION OF INVESTMENT RISK

How does the investment industry measure risk? What measures of risk do investors use to make decisions? Are the industry measures and peoples' preferences the same or even correlated? The answers to these questions are important for the investment industry, financial advisors, and our knowledge about investor behavior.

While the investment industry focuses on standard deviation as the primary measure of risk, investors may find other measures useful, like probability of a loss or magnitude of potential loss. To simulate an investment-like decision, a series of repeated gamble experiments were conducted. Consider the gamble where you have half a chance to win $200 and half a chance to lose $100. What does the distribution of outcomes look like if this gamble is repeated 50 times? What are the risks?

In a series of similar repeated gambles, participants were asked to estimate the standard deviation of outcomes, probability of loss, and average magnitude of a loss when one occurs. In addition, each person was asked to rate the riskiness of the repeated games on a scale of 1 to 100.[14] The subjects strongly overestimated the probability of a loss and had difficulty estimating the average loss magnitude when a loss occurred. The subjects also did a poor job of estimating the standard deviation, though there was no systematic over- or underestimation. Clearly, people have difficulty in quantifying risk. However, their risk rating (1 to 100) for each repeated gamble was positively correlated with the probability of loss and magnitude of loss. This suggests that investors do incorporate these risk measures into their own risk ratings. Unfortunately for the investment industry, standard deviation was not correlated with their judgment of risk.

Overall, people are not generally able to assess the statistics of outcome distributions. Therefore, people making decisions about their retirement investments may not be aware of the consequences of their actions.

MEMORY AND DECISION MAKING

Memory is not as much a factual recording of events as it is a perception of the physical and emotional experience. This perception is affected by the way in which the events unfold. The process that records events in the brain can store different features of the experience. These stored features are the basis for subsequent recall.

Memory has an adaptive function: It determines whether a situation experienced in the past should be desired or avoided in the future. For example, if you remember an experience as having been worse than it really was, you would be excessively motivated to avoid similar experiences. Alternatively, if you remember an experience as better than it was, you will invest too much effort in seeking similar experiences. Therefore, inaccurate perceptions of past experiences can lead to poor decisions.

Memory and Investment Decisions

This phenomenon can affect investors as well. The price pattern of a stock can affect how an investor makes decisions in the future. Consider this example of an investor purchasing two stocks. The investor buys the stock of a biotechnology firm and a pharmaceutical company. Each stock is purchased for $100.

Throughout the following year, the price of the biotechnology stock slowly declines to $75. The price of the pharmaceutical stock stays at $100 until the very end of the year, when it plunges to $80.

For the year, the biotechnology stock performed worse than the pharmaceutical stock. However, the two stocks lost money in different ways. The biotechnology stock experienced a gradual decline. The pharmaceutical stock experienced a dramatic loss at the end. The memory of the large loss at the end of the year is associated with a high degree of emotional pain. The memory of the slow loss creates less emotional pain. This can occur even though the biotechnology stock (the slow loser) performed worse. Therefore, when making decisions about these stocks for the following year, the investor might be overly pessimistic about the pharmaceutical stock.

This same pattern occurs for pleasurable experiences. People feel better about experiences with a high-pleasure peak and end. Consider a scenario in which the two stocks increased in price. The biotechnology stock slowly increased to $125 over the year. The pharmaceutical stock rose dramatically to $120 at the end of the year. The memory of these events causes the investor to feel better about the pharmaceutical stock even though it did not perform as well.

COGNITIVE DISSONANCE

Psychologists have studied specific consequences of memory problems. Consider that people typically view themselves as "smart and nice." Evidence that contradicts this image causes two seemingly opposite ideas. For example, suppose you want to think of yourself as nice, but the memory of one of your past actions suggests that you are not nice. Your brain would feel uncomfortable with this contradiction. Psychologists call this feeling *cognitive dissonance*. Simply stated, cognitive dissonance means that the brain is struggling with two opposite ideas—I am nice, but I am not nice. To avoid this psychological pain, people tend to ignore, reject, or minimize any information that conflicts with their positive self-image. Evidence that cannot be denied is accommodated by a change in beliefs.[15]

People's beliefs can change to be consistent with past decisions. We want to feel like we made the right decision. For example, racetrack gamblers were surveyed about the odds of "their horse" winning. Bettors just leaving the betting window gave their horse a better chance of winning than bettors standing in line to place their bets.[16] Before placing the bet, gamblers feel more uncertain about their chances. After placing the bet, their beliefs change to be consistent with their decision.

The avoidance of cognitive dissonance can affect the decision-making process in two ways. First, people may fail to make important decisions because it is too uncomfortable to contemplate the situation. For example, when considering the thought of saving for future retirement, some younger people may conjure an image of a feeble person with low earning power. To avoid the conflict between their good self-image and the contradictory future self-image, they avoid saving entirely. Second, the filtering of new information limits the ability to evaluate and monitor our investment decisions. If investors ignore negative information, how are they going to realize that an adjustment in their portfolio is necessary?

Cognitive Dissonance and Investing

Investors seek to reduce psychological pain by adjusting their beliefs about the success of past investment choices. For example, at one point in time, an investor will make a decision to purchase a mutual fund. Over time, performance information about the fund will make him or her either validate or put into question the wisdom of picking that mutual fund. To reduce cognitive dissonance, the investor's brain will filter out or reduce the negative information and fixate on the positive information. Therefore, investor memory of past performance is better than actual past performance. In other words, you view yourself as a good investor, so the memory of your past investment performance adapts to be consistent with the self-image. You remember that you have done well regardless of the actual performance.

William Goetzmann and Nadav Peles measured the recollections of investors.[17] They asked investors two questions about the return on their mutual fund investments during the previous year: (1) What was the return last year? (2) By how much did you beat the market? Note that these questions ask about actual performance and performance relative to possible alternatives. If investors are not biased by cognitive problems, then the average recollection of performance should be equal to the actual performance.

Goetzmann and Peles posed these questions to two groups of investors. The first group consisted of architects. Architects are highly educated professionals, but they might not be knowledgeable about investing. Twelve architects responded regarding 29 investments they owned through their defined contribution pension plan. Figure 4.1 shows the architects' errors in their recollections. On average, they recalled an investment performance that was 6.22 percent higher than their actual return. They thought they did much better than they actually did.

It is difficult to outperform the market. Most stock mutual funds cannot consistently beat the Standard & Poor's (S&P) 500 Index. So how did the architects think they did? On average, their estimate of how much they beat the market was 4.62 percent too optimistic. This group of investors overestimated their actual return and overestimated their return relative to a benchmark.

Responses from a second group of investors were collected from members of a state chapter of the American Association of Individual Investors (AAII). The AAII is an association that provides education, information, and services to individual investors. Presumably, the members of the AAII are well educated in investing. Do these investors overestimate their past returns?

Twenty-nine AAII members responded concerning 57 mutual funds they owned. These investors overestimated their past returns by 3.40 percent, on average. They overestimated their performance relative to the market by 5.11 percent. Even though these people are educated investors, they are also overly optimistic in recalling their past returns.

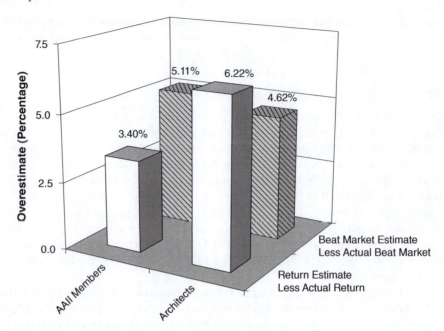

FIGURE 4.1 Errors in Memory (Cognitive Dissonance)

Markus Glaser and Martin Weber asked online German investors about their annual returns from 1997 to 2000.[18] They compared each response to the actual annualized return from the investors' brokerage accounts. Figure 4.2 shows that the mean difference between the estimated return and actual return was over 10 percent. The investors overestimated their performance by 11.6 percent. Unfortunately, experienced investors did not remember their return much better. Low-experience investors overestimated by 13.2 percent, while the more-experienced investors overestimated by 10.3 percent. Glaser and Weber concluded that investors will have difficulty learning from their mistakes if they do not know or remember those mistakes.

Also consider the responses of investors in a simulated market experiment.[19] The performance of ten real mutual funds, a money market fund, and the S&P 500 Index over the 10-year period of 1985–1994 were used in the simulation. Eighty master's-level business students allocated $100,000 to the investments as they wanted. Then six-month returns were revealed to the investors, and they could reallocate their portfolios. This was repeated until 20 turns of the game were completed. Note that throughout the experiment, the players saw the market return (as proxied by the S&P 500 Index) and their own portfolio holdings. After the game, the players were asked how they performed: What return did they get? Did they beat the market? On average, the players reported that they beat the market. This is a rosy perception of their performance because the group's average return was 8 percent below the market. When asked about their returns, only 15 of the 80 were correct. A majority (47 out of 80) overestimated their total return.

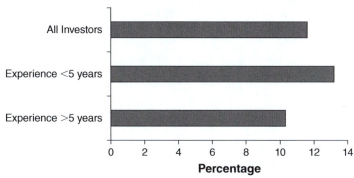

FIGURE 4.2   Overestimation of Past Returns by Online Investors in Germany

People want to believe that their investment decisions are good. In the face of evidence to the contrary, the brain's defense mechanisms filter contradictory information and alter the recollection of the decision. It is hard to objectively evaluate the progress toward investment goals or the need for an investment advisor when the recollection of past performance is biased upward.

NATURE OR NURTURE?

So far, this chapter has focused on the investor environment as the main factor for determining risk aversion. For example, an investor's education, level of wealth, and recent experience investing are factors in his desire to take risk. These are examples of how nurture impacts our investment decisions. What about nature? Does your genetic makeup influence your decisions?

Several studies try to examine to what degree biology impacts risk aversion through the behavior of twins—both identical and nonidentical twins. Consider three studies that use three different methods: surveys, experiments, and actual financial asset holdings. For example, one study asked twins three survey questions about various potential gambles. These questions allowed the authors to compute a risk aversion measure. They then determine the determining factors of the variation in risk aversion between people. A subject's risk aversion might be due to his nurture variables, or it might be related to the risk aversion of his twin. Their conclusions are profound: "Risk preferences appear to be coded in the human genome as our results show that economic risk preferences are two-thirds genetically and one-third environmentally determined."[20] Using an experimental design, another paper estimates that 20 percent of the variation in risk aversion is due to genetics.[21]

Lastly, one paper examines the financial portfolio of over 37,000 twins and an equal sample of nontwins, all from Sweden.[22] They examine three choices that indicate a person's level of risk aversion: (1) whether they have invested in the stock market, (2) the portion of their portfolio invested in the stock market, and (3) the level of risk in the portfolio as measured by volatility. They report that genetics explain about a third of the decision differences seen between people. This is a larger proportion than is explained by individual characteristics like age, gender, education, and wealth *combined*!

Summary

Although we often think of some people as bigger risk takers than others, our risk aversion and risk tolerance is more dependent on previous successes and failures. People tend to increase their tolerance for risk after big gains (house-money effect) and after losses when there is a chance to break even. Otherwise, losses lead to reduced risk exposure. However, genetics (or nature) play just as large a role as individual characteristics and past experience in explaining someone's level of risk aversion.

When many investors are affected by these problems, the entire market can be affected.

The psychological bias of seeking (or ignoring) risk because of the house-money effect contributes to the creation of a price bubble. The psychological bias of avoiding risk in the snakebite effect leads to stock prices that are driven too low after the bubble collapses.

Also, human memory is more a recording of emotions and feelings of events than a recording of facts. This can cause investors to remember actual events inaccurately or even to ignore information that causes bad feelings. Misreading and overestimating prior performance will make it difficult to learn from mistakes.

Questions

1. Television shows on poker have become popular on television. The programs follow the action of no-limit hold-'em tournaments. You might observe that after winning a big pot, many gamblers bet the next hand even when they have poor cards. After losing a big hand, many gamblers tend not to bet the next hand even when they have good cards. Explain these two behaviors.
2. Describe the appeal of "double-or-nothing" gambles. Be sure to include reference points (from Chapter 3).
3. How does the flow of news and information impact the memory process to cause investors to remember a "rosy" view of past portfolio performance?
4. Explain who should have more similar levels of risk aversion, identical twins or nonidentical twins. How would raising twins apart from each other affect the similarity of their portfolios?

Notes

1. From Daniel Kahneman and Amos Tversky, "Prospect Theory: An Analysis of Decisions Under Risk," *Econometrica* 47(1979): 287. © Econometric Society.
2. This discussion is adapted from Richard Thaler and Eric Johnson, "Gambling with the House Money and Trying to Break Even: The Effects of Prior Outcomes on Risky Choice," *Management Science* 36(1990): 643–660.
3. Daniel Kahneman and Amos Tversky, "Prospect Theory: An Analysis of Decisions Under Risk," *Econometrica* 47(1979): 263–291.
4. Thierry Post, Martijn van den Assem, Guido Baltussen, and Richard Thaler, "Deal or No Deal? Decision Making Under Risk in a Large-Payoff Game Show," *American Economic Review* 98(2008): 38–71.

5. Joshua Coval and Tyler Shumway, "Do Behavioral Biases Affect Prices?" *Journal of Finance* 60(2005): 1–34.

6. Massimo Massa and Andrei Simonov, "Behavioral Biases and Investment," *Review of Finance* 9(2005): 483–507.

7. Tracey Longo, "Stupid Investor Tricks," *Financial Planning* (April 2000): 116.

8. Richard Thaler, "Toward a Positive Theory of Consumer Choice," *Journal of Economic Behavior and Organization* 1(1980): 39–60.

9. William Samuelson and Richard Zeckhauser, "Status Quo Bias in Decision Making," *Journal of Risk and Uncertainty* 1(1988): 7–59.

10. Daniel Kahneman, Jack Knetsch, and Richard Thaler, "Experimental Tests of the Endowment Effect and the Coase Theorem," *Journal of Political Economy* 98(1990): 1325–1348, and "Anomalies: The Endowment Effect, Loss Aversion, and Status Quo Bias," *Journal of Economic Perspectives* 1(1991): 193–206.

11. George Lowenstein and Daniel Kahneman, "Explaining the Endowment Effect," Carnegie Mellon University working paper (1991).

12. John List, "Does Market Experience Eliminate Market Anomalies?" *Quarterly Journal of Economics* 118(2003): 41–71.

13. William Samuelson and Richard Zeckhauser, "Status Quo Bias in Decision Making," *Journal of Risk and Uncertainty* 1(1988): 7–59.

14. Alexander Klos, Elke Weber, and Martin Weber, "Investment Decisions and Time Horizon: Risk Perception and Risk Behavior in Repeated Gambles," *Management Science* (2005): 1777–1790.

15. The description of cognitive dissonance comes from George Akerlof and William Dickens, "The Economic Consequences of Cognitive Dissonance," *American Economic Review* 72(1982): 307–319.

16. Robert Knox and James Inkster, "Postdecision Dissonance at Post Time," *Journal of Personality and Social Psychology* 8(1968): 319–323.

17. William Goetzmann and Nadav Peles, "Cognitive Dissonance and Mutual Fund Investors," *Journal of Financial Research* 20(1997): 145–158.

18. Markus Glaser and Martin Weber, "Why Inexperienced Investors Do Not Learn: They Do Not Know Their Past Portfolio Performance," *Finance Research Letters* 4(2007): 203–216.

19. Don Moore, Terri Kurtzberg, Craig Fox, and Max Bazerman, "Positive Illusions and Forecasting Errors in Mutual Fund Investment Decisions," *Organizational Behavior and Human Decision Processes* 79(1999): 95–114.

20. Michael J. Zyphur, Jayanth Narayanan, Richard D. Arvey, and Gordon J. Alexander, "The Genetics of Economic Risk Preferences," *Journal of Behavioral Decision Making* 22(2009): 367–377.

21. David Cesarini, Christopher T. Dawes, Magnus Johannesson, Paul Lichtenstein, and Bjorn Wallace, "Genetic Variation in Preferences for Giving and Risk Taking," *Quarterly Journal of Economics* 124(2011): 809–842.

22. Amir Barnea, Henrik Cronqvist, and Stephan Siegel, "Nature or Nurture: What Determines Investor Behavior?" *Journal of Financial Economics* 98(2010): 583–604.

Decision Frames

The way in which a question is asked has a strong impact on the answer given or decision made. Consider the case of opting-in versus opting-out. To consent to be an organ donor in the United States, you must sign a paper when getting your driver's license. The consent is then noted on the license. This is an opt-in decision chosen by only about a quarter of drivers. The levels are even lower for countries like Germany and the United Kingdom.[1] On the other hand, a program can be designed in which every driver is automatically defaulted to be a donor. People not wishing to be an organ donor must sign a paper to opt out. The participation rate of organ donor consent in opt-out countries (like Austria, France, and Sweden) is typically in the high 90-percent range. The simple decision frame of having people opt out instead of opt in dramatically raises the participation rate.

FRAMING AND CHOICE

One very popular example of framing comes from Nobel Laureate Daniel Kahneman about choosing a program to battle a disease outbreak:[2]

Imagine that the United States is preparing for the outbreak of an unusual disease, which is expected to kill 600 people. Two alternative programs to combat the disease have been proposed. Assume the exact scientific estimates of the consequences of the programs are as follows:

> *If program A is adopted, 200 people will be saved.*

> *If program B is adopted, there is a 1/3 probability that 600 people will be saved, and a 2/3 probability that no one will be saved.*

> *Which program would you choose?*

Participants in the experiment are asked to choose a program. Now consider the altered programs:

The same disease is back. Only this time the two programs now have the following payoffs:

   If program C is adopted, 400 people will die.

   If program D is adopted, there is a 1/3 probability that nobody will die, and a 2/3 probability that 600 people will die.

   Which program would you support?

Participants are asked which of these two programs should be chosen. This is an example of positive and negative versions of framing. You may have noticed that program A and program C are the same programs. In both cases, 400 people will live and 200 people will die. The difference is that program A is framed in a positive manner—people living. Program C has a negative frame by describing the deaths. In addition, programs C and D are the same, except for the positive/negative frame.

   If people are not impacted by the frame of the question, then the same proportion of people who pick program A in the positive frame would pick program C if given the negative frame. But this did not turn out to be the case, as 72 percent of the people who were shown the positive frame picked the certain results in program A and only 28 percent picked the risky program B. When thinking about saving lives, most people did not want to take a risk. But when the negative frame was shown, only 22 percent picked the certain program C and 78 percent chose the risky program D. Note that in the negative frame, participants were far more interested in the risky program. People make different choices depending on the frame of the question posed.

   The previous example included an emotional topic, namely people living or dying. Do framing effects occur in nonemotional settings? Multiplication may be the least emotional mental process! Consider the experiment in which participants were given 10 seconds to estimate the following problem: $2 \times 3 \times 4 \times 5 \times 6 \times 7 \times 8$. Another group of participants were given the problem: $8 \times 7 \times 6 \times 5 \times 4 \times 3 \times 2$. These are obviously the same problems with the twist that the numbers are arranged in the opposite order.[3] Should the order (or frame) impact the estimate? Estimates from groups that estimated the first version averaged 512. Estimates for groups estimating the second version averaged 2,250. People came up with estimates more than four times higher simply because they anchored to the higher number 8 versus the lower number 2. By the way, people did not estimate very well as the answer is 40,320.

FRAMING AND INVESTING

Framing and the Risk-Return Relationship

It is clear that the framing of a question influences the choices made. How might framing impact investment choices? The most fundamental principle in finance is the positive relationship between risk and expected return. Investors can expect higher returns from high-risk investments and low returns from low-risk ones. Indeed, while asset pricing models might measure risk in different ways, they all require a positive risk premium to be associated with risk. Every student and practitioner of finance knows to demand a higher return in order to invest in a higher-risk stock.

There are potentially many types of risk for the stock market investor. Two firm characteristics that are considered to be associated with risk are the firm's leverage and growth prospects. A firm that uses more debt in its capital structure is considered to have more leverage and thus be riskier. Firms with poor growth prospects are often identified by their high book-to-market (B/M) ratio, which is related to the B/M risk factor in some asset pricing models. In a randomized survey experiment, 742 Finnish financial advisors are asked about the return of firms with these risky characteristics in two different frames.[4]

One frame asks about the risk premium demanded for firms with these leverage and growth characteristics. If the advisor believes that these are risk factors, then that advisor should respond that a risk premium is needed. Those advisors with this frame overwhelmingly responded that a risk premium is demanded—77.7 percent required the premium for poor growth firms, and 86.2 percent required the premium for highly leveraged firms. With this added risk premium, the return expected will be higher for these higher-risk firms. This is consistent with the positive risk-return relationship. The other advisors were asked the question from a different frame. They were simply asked if firms with these characteristics would have higher, lower, or the same returns as firms without leverage and poor growth. In this frame, only 1.9 percent of the advisors believed that poor-growth firms would earn a higher return. Only 12.5 percent believed higher-leverage firms would earn a higher return. In this frame, the advisors projected a *negative* risk-return relationship, which is the opposite of both financial theory and of the advisors answering from the first frame. Figure 5.1 shows the comparison of responses between the two frames.

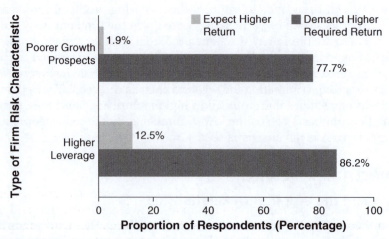

FIGURE 5.1   Financial Advisor View of Risk and Return in Two Different Frames

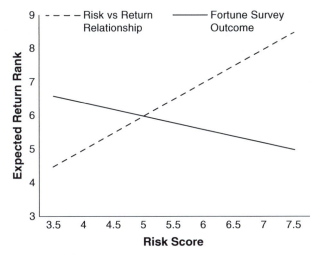

FIGURE 5.2   Executive and Analyst Risk and Return Perspectives

Another example of the failure to apply the positive risk-return relationship occurs in a survey of high net-worth clients of a U.S. investment firm.[5] They were given a list of 210 firms from the annual *Fortune* survey of executives and analysts. Some of the investors were asked to denote the riskiness of each firm on a scale of 1 (low) to 10 (high). The others ranked the future return of each firm. Putting the two groups' responses together produced the positive risk-return relationship shown in the dashed line in Figure 5.2. That is, firms generally considered to be riskier should also be expected to have a higher return—Low-risk firms should be expected to provide low future returns. However, the responses reflected the solid line in the figure. High-risk firms were also expected to provide low returns.

Why do people who understand (and even agree with) the positive risk-return relationship often fail to apply that relationship? It is because of framing. When people frame the situation within a risk-return context, they usually get it right. But when they use a different frame, they fail to follow this relationship. Indeed, without expressly framing risk and return together, investors often use a frame of better/worse instead. Investors tend to think of stocks as better or worse. Better stocks have high returns and low risk. Worse stocks have low returns and high risk. Unfortunately, the better/worse frame does not describe the risk-return relationship accurately, and thus investors often take more risk than they know.

Framing and Prediction

Consider this question: If the Dow Jones Industrial Average had risen 20 percent last year to 8,000, what *level* do you estimate it will achieve at the end of this year? Now consider this slight change in the question: If the Dow Jones Industrial Average had risen to 8,000 last year, what *return* do you estimate it will provide this year?

These two questions are asking for the same prediction, but the first asks for a price forecast while the second asks for a return forecast. While this may seem trivial, it is not. In this scenario, people responding to the price version of the question would give an answer that is lower than implied by the people forecasting the return. A group of German scholars showed that when people identify a stock price trend and are asked to predict the future, they tend to extrapolate the trend (a representativeness bias) when responding in terms of changes or returns.[6] Those people responding in the price-level mode tend to show a slowing or even reversal of the trend that can be considered a mean-reversion approach.

Forecasting is popular in finance and economics. Many organizations survey people asking for future returns, like the Michigan survey of consumers, Duke/CFO (chief financial officer) Business Outlook Survey, and UBS/Gallup. Other organizations ask for future prices, like the Livingston Survey of the Federal Reserve Bank of Philadelphia. Analysts also provide price targets on the stocks they follow. This return/price framing bias suggests that outlooks from return forecasts will be biased toward extending the current trend while price forecasts will tend more toward a belief in mean reversion.

When investors pick one stock instead of others, they are essentially making a prediction about that firm's risk and return relative to the others. In addition, a factor to framing that impacts prediction is the intelligence of the decision maker. Three scholars illustrate the role of intelligence in a data set of Finnish investors in which they have IQ information from prior (mandatory) military service.[7] They find that the high IQ investors' portfolios outperform the low IQ investors by 4.9 percent per year. This higher return stems from the higher IQ investors exhibiting better market timing and stock picking. In addition, they are less prone to the disposition effect and the sentiment of other investors.

THINKING MODE AND DECISION PROCESSES

In Daniel Kahneman's Nobel lecture delivered in Stockholm when he received the Bank of Sweden Prize in Economic Sciences, he outlined two different modes of cognitive reasoning.[8] He describes the analytical thinking mode (what he calls reasoning) as what we do "when we compute the product of 17 and 258." On the other hand, the *intuitive* thinking mode is used when you are reluctant to eat a piece of chocolate that has been formed in the shape of a cockroach. The intuitive mode is spontaneous and effortless while analytical thought is deliberate and effortful.

Consider the example of driving a car while talking on a cell phone. Most drivers can carry on a conversation when the discussion is minor chitchat and the driving requires only effortless cognitive processing. These intuitive activities can occur together because the brain can handle these cognitive processes in parallel. However, problems arise when the conversation and/or driving task requires more analytical processing (like a political debate or parallel parking). These analytically dominated activities require the brain to process in a more serial manner. Thus, either the conversation becomes interrupted or the driving does. Due to its effortless aspects, most judgments and choices are made intuitively.

However, many investment decisions require assessing uncertainty and risk, abstract ideas that could require significant cognitive effort. These decisions should also occur within the context of financial theory, like diversification, asset allocation, market efficiency, and risk versus expected return. It is likely that people who predominately make decisions using the intuitive mode might make different financial choices than those who predominately use the analytical mode.

In addition, thinking mode may impact how people view decision frames. For example, consider the gambler at a horse track who brought $150 and has lost $140 of it. The gambler is considering betting the last $10 on a 15-to-1 long shot.[9] How is this decision framed? One could frame the decision in the positive frame of a choice between keeping $10 for certain or taking a risk with a low probability to win $150 and high probability to get nothing. On the other hand, the gambler could consider the negative frame of losing $140 on the day for certain versus a risk of a high chance of losing $150 for the day and a small chance of breaking even. Both frames are legitimate ways of thinking about the decision. However, prospect theory suggests people tend to take the certain option in the positive frame (keeping the $10 and not making the 15:1 long-shot bet) and take the risky option in the negative frame (making the long-shot bet). Thus, how the gambler frames this decision will have a large impact on the decision made.

MEASURING THINKING MODE

Shane Frederick introduced three quick and simple questions called the cognitive reflection test (CRT) to measure the intuitive/analytical thinking mode.[10] The questions are designed such that the correct answer requires a more deliberate approach. However, there is an impulsive answer that quickly comes to mind. The intuitive thinker will pick this impulsive (but incorrect) answer while the analytical thinker deliberates a little longer to find the correct answer. The questions are:

If it takes 5 machines 5 minutes to make 5 widgets, how long would it take 100 machines to make 100 widgets? (impulsive answer is 100 minutes; correct answer is 5 minutes)

In a lake, there is a patch of lily pads. Every day, the patch doubles in size. If it takes 48 days for the patch to cover the entire lake, how long would it take for the patch to cover half the lake? (impulsive answer is 24 days; correct answer is 47 days)

A bat and ball together cost $1.10. The bat costs $1.00 more than the ball. How much does the ball cost? (impulsive answer is 10 cents; correct answer is 5 cents)

The CRT measure is the number of correct answers. Therefore, a CRT score of 0 or 1 indicates an intuitive thinker while 2 and 3 denote an analytical thinker. Professor Frederick reports that Massachusetts Institute of Technology students averaged a CRT score of 2.18. It is not surprising that students at one of the top engineering schools in the world would lean toward being analytical. A choir group at Harvard University averaged 1.43 and an online study averaged 1.1. I believe that Internet activities tend toward quick, intuitive thinking processes.

RISK FRAMING AND THINKING STYLE

Like the gambler at the horse track discussed earlier, people may face decisions framed in the positive or negative. The infectious-disease example at the beginning of this chapter illustrates that people often make different choices when faced with the two frames. In general, prospect theory describes the tendency for people to choose the certain option when framed in a positive domain and choose the risky option when framed in the negative domain. Professor Frederick reports that students with low CRT scores behave in a manner more consistent with the axioms of prospect theory than students with high CRT scores. He asks many versions of the questions in the gain domain, *"Which investment payoff would you pick? Receive (A) $100 for certain or (B) a 50% chance to receive $300 and a 50% to receive nothing."* Note that the certain payoff of $100 is less than the expected value of the gamble ($150), which might be considered to include a risk premium. In addition, the loss domain questions were in the form of, *"Which investment payoff would you pick? Lose (A) $100 for certain or (B) a 50% chance to pay $300 and a 50% chance to pay nothing."* Here, the certain alternative has a higher expected value than the gamble.

Frederick found that low-CRT-score students picked A in the positive domain and B in the negative domain. High-CRT-score students did the opposite. But what about better-trained and more-experienced investors, do they behave in the same manner? I tested over 100 financial planners to find out.[11]

Figure 5.3 shows the portion of financial planners, grouped by thinking mode, who selected the certain and risky options in the positive (Gain) domain.

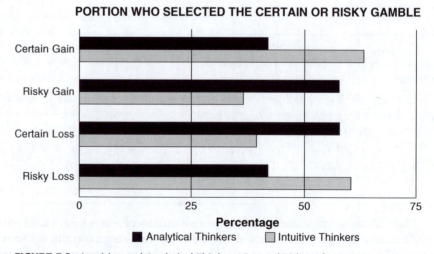

PORTION WHO SELECTED THE CERTAIN OR RISKY GAMBLE

FIGURE 5.3   Intuitive and Analytical Thinkers' Framed Risk Preferences

Notice that more than half of the intuitive thinkers wanted the certain $100 while a majority of the analytical planners wanted to take the gamble. In the loss domain, both groups switched. More than half of the analytical planners settled for paying the certain $100, while more than half of the intuitive planners wanted the chance to break even.

This figure shows two important behavioral findings. First, people do not have one risk-aversion level. Instead, they may be risk seeking in one frame and risk averse in another. Second, intuitive thinkers behave along the axioms of prospect theory, while analytical thinkers do not.

FRAMING FINANCIAL DECISIONS

We must constantly make decisions regarding which products to buy. It is no accident that we often have a choice from three options. Do you want a Tall, Grande, or Venti latte? We like our questions framed in such a way that we can easily compare. The rational economic decision maker was first purported to make the value maximizing decision. But it appears now that we actually make many of our decisions based on *extremeness aversion*.

Extremeness aversion is demonstrated by Amos Tversky, cocreator of prospect theory, and colleague Itamar Simonson.[12] Consider the purchase decision between two cameras: (1) Minolta X-370 for $169.99 or (2) Minolta Maximum 3000i for $239.99. Given these two choices, 50 percent of the people pick the cheaper camera and 50 percent pick the more expensive one. But when a third, more expensive camera is offered (Minolta Maximum 7000i for $469.99), 22 percent pick the cheaper priced camera, 57 percent pick the middle priced one, and 21 percent pick the expensive camera. Note that half of the people that would pick the cheap camera with only two offered end up picking a more expensive camera when a third high priced camera is offered. This is because extremeness aversion causes us to avoid the most extreme appearing options. The cheapest camera does not appear extreme with only one other alternative. It does look "cheap" when compared to two more expensive alternatives.

Pension Decisions

Some of the most important decisions that impact peoples' future wealth are their pension plan decisions. Workers with a defined contribution plan must decide whether to contribute, how much to contribute, and how to allocate the investment to various asset classes. Given how important pension plans are to both individuals and to society, do we frame the decisions in ways that will foster optimal choices? Unfortunately, the answer is no. Traditionally, the new employee receives a thick packet of information and is told to return to the human resources office when they are ready to make their choices. A majority never come back.

What framing problems are typical in a 401(k) pension plan? One issue is that employees really do know what level of risk is appropriate for them. Since they are unsure, they tend to be extremeness averse. Shlomo Benartzi and

TABLE 5.1 Extremeness Aversion in Risk Choices

	Option A	Option B	Option C	Option D
First Frame				
Good Market Conditions: 50% chance	$900	$1,100	$1,260	
Bad Market Conditions: 50% chance	$900	$800	$700	
Second Frame				
Good Market Conditions: 50% chance		$1,100	$1,260	$1,380
Bad Market Conditions: 50% chance		$800	$700	$600

Data Source: Shlomo Benartzi and Richard Thaler, "How Much Is Investor Autonomy Worth?" *Journal of Finance* (2002): 57, 1593–1616.

Richard Thaler illustrate this with their experiments asking people which risk profiles they prefer.[13] In the first framing of the question, Options A, B, and C are offered (see Table 5.1). When these three investment alternatives are offered, only 29.2 percent of the people preferred C over B. Is this just because most people feel that Option B is a better fit for them? Consider that the second frame offers Options B, C, and D. If people know their optimal level of risk, then most should still prefer B to C. However, in this frame, 53.8 percent of the people preferred C over B. Why do most people change their preference from B in the first frame to C in the second frame? It is because these are the alternatives that appear less extreme within their respective questions. People don't know what level of risk they should take, so they pick the one they perceive as moderate.

Another problem is the opt-in nature of the plans. Consider the organ donor program discussed at the opening of this chapter. Programs where drivers must opt out of the organ donor program have a much higher organ donor volunteer rate than programs that require drivers to opt in. An analysis of one 401(k) plan transitioning from the traditional opt-in design to a new opt-out design found that the participation rate of new employees skyrocketed from 37 percent to 86 percent.[14] The new framing of the decision to participate had a dramatic impact.

Another problem is the number of options available for investment allocation in pension plans. Even grocery shoppers can get overwhelmed by the number of choices available. For example, a store display of 6 flavors of jam results in more purchases than a display of 24 flavors of jam. Employees can also get overwhelmed when they have hundreds of investment choices in their pension plan. An overwhelmed employee delays making decisions so long that he or she never ends up participating in the plan. One study shows that the probability of participation by an employee falls by 1.5–2 percent for every 10 mutual funds added to the menu. Having fewer funds to choose from leads to higher participation.[15]

The opt-in/opt-out choice and the number of investment alternatives are just two of the framing issues being studied in pension-plan design.

Payday Loans

A good example of manipulating behavior through frames occurs at Payday lenders. Signs nudge borrowers to think in narrow frames. For example, large signs declare that financing fees of $15 are charged per $100 borrowed. Loans are typically for two weeks. However, borrowers average over $350 in loan size and also average more than 9 loans before finally paying off the debt. Can restating the facts help borrowers view the loan from a more broad frame and impact their desire to pay down the loan quicker?

This question is tested by Marianne Bertrand and Adair Morse at the University of Chicago. They survey borrowers after they have received a loan, asking the borrowers for questions about themselves and the purpose of the loan.[16] Other information is obtained from the Payday lender. The randomized experiment occurs by the loan cash being placed in different envelopes with printed facts. The control group envelopes are the Payday company standard logo and store information. The other envelopes display information on either: (1) the true dollar cost of a $300 loan over a variety of time periods, (2) the annual percentage rate of the payday loan compared to other types of loans, or (3) the distribution of the time it takes people to pay back the loan.

They find that the strongest frame displays the dollar cost, but all three reduce the likelihood of the borrower taking out another payday loan. Compared to the control sample, recasting the loan information to influence a broader frame decreased the number of borrowers who take out another payday loan by 11 percent. This has policy implications for laws about loan disclosures on all types of subprime lending.

Summary

People seem to be fooled by decision frames. That is, the choices they make are influenced by the frame of the question. One such frame is the positive/negative context. Whether the frame or context is people saved versus deaths or profits versus losses, people prefer the low-risk option in the positive frame and the risky alternative in the negative frame, which is predicted by prospect theory.

Thinking mode may also be a factor. Intuitive decision makers behave in a manner consistent with prospect theory. However, those who use a more analytical process often do not. Thus, frames may influence people differently.

Frames impact investors too. The current design of many 401(k) plans use decision frames like the opt-in procedure and many investment menu choices that do not foster plan participation. Better designs can help people make better choices. However, note that the frame we see the most often in the media is one of a very short-term focus. The attention of TV, newspapers, and the Internet is always on how much the market moved *today*. We rarely are put into the frame of how asset classes have moved in the last 10 years. It helps to reframe information in broader terms, whether it be investment focus, pension choices, or payday lending.

Questions

1. When investors think of an investment as better or worse, how is it viewed differently from the risk-return relationship view? How might it impact an investor's portfolio?

2. Speculate how an intuitive thinker's investment decisions and portfolio might be different from an analytical investor's.

3. Give an example of how extreme aversion nudges you toward various consumer choices.

4. If participating in a defined contribution plan is good for employees, what framing characteristics might impede participation? How could they be changed?

5. How does narrow framing of loan characteristics impact borrowers' decision?

Notes

1. Eric J. Johnson and Daniel Goldstein, "Do Defaults Save Lives?" *Science* (2003): 1338–1339.

2. Amos Tversky and Daniel Kahneman, "The Framing of Decisions and the Psychology of Choice," *Science* 211(1981): 453–458.

3. Amos Tversky and Daniel Kahneman, "Judgment under Uncertainty: Heuristics and Biases," *Science* 185(1974): 1124–1131.

4. Markku Kaustia, Heidi Laukkanen, and Vesa Puttonen, "Should Good Stocks Have High Prices or High Returns?" *Financial Analysts Journal* 65(2009): 55–62.

5. Meir Statman, Kenneth L. Fisher, and Deniz Anginer, "Affect in a Behavioral Asset-Pricing Model," *Financial Analysts Journal* 64(2008): 20–29.

6. Markus Glaser, Thomas Langer, Jens Reynolds, and Martin Weber, "Framing Effects in Stock Market Forecasts: The Difference Between Asking for Prices and Asking for Returns," *Review of Finance* 11(2007): 325–357.

7. Mark Grinblatt, Matti Keloharju, and Juhani T. Linnainmaa, "IQ, Trading Behavior, and Performance," *Journal of Financial Economics* 104(2012): 339–362.

8. Daniel Kahneman, "Maps of Bounded Rationality: Psychology for Behavioral Economics," *American Economic Review* 93(2003): 1449–1475.

9. Amos Tversky and Daniel Kahneman, "The Framing of Decisions and the Psychology of Choice," *Science* 211(1981): 453–458.

10. Shane Frederick, "Cognitive Reflection and Decision Making," *Journal of Economic Perspectives* 19(2005): 25–42.

11. John Nofsinger and Abhishek Varma, "How Analytical Is Your Financial Advisor?" *Financial Services Review* 16(2007): 245–260.

12. Itamar Simonson and Amos Tversky, "Choice in Context: Tradeoff Contrast and Extremeness Aversion," *Journal of Marketing Research* 29(1992): 281–295.

13. Shlomo Benartzi and Richard Thaler, "How Much Is Investor Autonomy Worth?" *Journal of Finance* 57(2002): 1593–1616.

14. Brigitte Madrian and Dennis F. Shea, "The Power of Suggestion: Inertia in 401(k) Participation and Savings Behavior," *Quarterly Journal of Economics* 116(2001): 1149–1187.

15. See Sheena Iyengar and Mark Lepper, "When Choice Is Demotivating: Can One Desire Too Much of a Good Thing?" *Journal of Personality and Social Psychology* 79(2000): 995–1006; and Sheena Sethi-Iyengar, Gur Huberman, and Wei Jiang, "How Much Choice Is Too Much? Contributions to 401(k) Retirement Plans," *Pension Design and Structure: New Lessons from Behavioral Finance,* Edited by Olivia Mitchell and Stephen Utkus, Oxford University Press, 83–95.

16. Marianne Bertrand and Adair Morse, "Information Disclosure, Cognitive Biases, and Payday Borrowing," *Journal of Finance* 66(2011): 1865–1893.

Mental Accounting

Businesses, governments, and even churches use accounting systems to track, separate, and categorize the flow of money. People, on the other hand, use a mental accounting system. Imagine that your brain uses a mental accounting system similar to a file cabinet. Each decision, action, and outcome is placed in a separate folder in the file cabinet. The folder contains the costs and benefits associated with a particular decision. Once an outcome is assigned to a mental folder, it is difficult to view that outcome in any other way. The ramifications of mental accounting are that it influences your decisions in unexpected ways.

Consider the following example.[1]

Mr. and Mrs. J have saved $15,000 toward their dream vacation home. They hope to buy the home in five years. The money earns 4 percent in a money market account. They just bought a new car for $11,000 that they financed with a three-year car loan at 9 percent.

This is a common situation. People have money in savings that earns a low rate of return yet borrow money at a high interest rate, thus losing money. In this example, the vacation home savings in the money market account is earning a rate of 4 percent. Imagine how excited Mr. and Mrs. J would be if they found a safe investment earning 9 percent! But when the 9 percent opportunity came up, they probably didn't even consider it. That opportunity was to borrow the $11,000 from their own savings (instead of the bank) and pay themselves a 9 percent interest rate. If they had done this, the vacation home savings in the money market account would have been more than $1,000 higher at the end of the three years.

Money does not come with labels, so people put labels on it. We have designations like dirty money, easy money, free money, and so on. Mr. and Mrs. J labeled their savings as "vacation home" in a mental account. Although mixing the "new car" mental account with the "vacation home" account would have maximized their wealth, Mr. and Mrs. J could not bring themselves to do it.

MENTAL BUDGETING

People use financial budgets to keep track of and control their spending. The brain uses mental budgets to associate the benefits of consumption with the costs in each mental account. Consider the pain (or costs) associated with the purchase of goods and services to be similar to that of the pain of financial losses. Similarly, the joy (or benefits) of consuming the goods and services is like the joy of financial gains. Mental budgeting matches the emotional pain to the emotional joy.

Matching Costs to Benefits

People usually prefer a "pay-as-you-go" payment system because it provides a tight match between the benefits and costs of the purchase. However, things get more complicated when the pay-as-you-go system is not available.

Consider the following set of questions that investigate the timing of payments. Professors Drazen Prelec and George Loewenstein asked 91 visitors to the Phipps Conservatory in Pittsburgh the following questions.[2] The first question was as follows:

Imagine that six months from now, you are planning to purchase a clothes washer and dryer for your new residence. The two machines together will cost $1,200. You have two options for financing the washer/dryer:

A. Six monthly payments of $200 each during the six months before the washer and dryer arrive.
B. Six monthly payments of $200 each during the six months beginning after the washer and dryer arrive.

Which option would you choose? Note that the total cost is the same in both options; only the timing of the costs is different. Of the 91 people interviewed, 84 percent responded that they preferred the postponed payment schedule B. This is consistent with the cost/benefit matching of mental budgeting. The benefits of the washer and dryer will be used for a period of years after their purchase. Paying the cost over a concurrent period matches the cost to the benefit. Note that option B is also consistent with traditional economic theories; that is, people should choose B because it is less expensive after considering the time value of money.

The next two examples are not consistent with traditional economic theories, and respondents did not select the wealth-maximizing option. Consider this example.

Imagine that you are planning to take a one-week vacation to the Caribbean six months from now. The vacation will cost $1,200. You have two options for financing the vacation:

A. Six monthly payments of $200 each during the six months before the vacation.

B. Six monthly payments of $200 each during the six months beginning after you return.

Notice that the payment stream options are the same as in the prior question—six payments before or six payments after the purchase. The change is that the item being purchased has changed. The main difference is that the vacation is a purchase whose benefits will be consumed in a short time, whereas the benefits of the washer and dryer will be consumed over the course of years. Which option would you choose?

Sixty percent of the respondents selected option A, the prepaid vacation. In this case, the payment options do not match with the consumption of the goods. The benefits of vacations are consumed during the vacation, but this vacation must be paid for either before or afterward.

Traditional economic theories predict that people will prefer option B because it is cheaper after considering the time value of money. However, most people choose option A. Why? People believe that a prepaid vacation is more pleasurable than one that must be paid for later because the pain of payment is over. If payment is to be made later, the benefits of the vacation are diminished by wondering how much the pleasure is going to cost. An important factor in the "prepay or finance it" decision is the amount of pleasure expected to be generated by the purchase. The thought of paying for an item over the time that the item is being used reduces the pleasure of using that item. But let's face it: Using a washer and dryer is not that much fun anyway, so we might as well finance it. The dream home example at the beginning of this chapter is another matter. The pleasure of the dream home should not be tainted with debt and the thoughts of future payments; therefore, Mr. and Mrs. J are prepaying (saving for) the house.

The third question to the visitors addressed income from overtime work to be performed: How would you like to get paid for working a few hours on the weekends during the next six months? Prepayment for work to be done in the future was not desirable. Sixty-six percent of the respondents preferred to get paid after doing the work instead of before. Again, this is not consistent with traditional economic theories. The wealth-maximizing option is to get paid earlier, not later.

Matching Debt

In the vacation and overtime questions, people are expressing an aversion to debt when the good or service is consumed quickly. People show a preference for matching the length of the payments to the length of time the good or service is used. For example, using debt to purchase homes, cars, TVs, and so forth is popular because these items are consumed over many years. Using debt and paying off the purchase over time results in a strong match associated with the consumption of those items.

On the other hand, people do not like to make payments on a debt for a purchase that has already been consumed. Financing the vacation is undesirable because it causes a long-term cost on a short-term benefit. This is also true for the third question. People do not want to get prepaid for work because it creates a long-term debt (working weekends for the next six months) for a short-term benefit (getting paid). People prefer to do the work first and then get paid.

SUNK-COST EFFECT

Traditional economic theories predict that people will consider the present and future costs and benefits when determining a course of action. Past costs should not be a factor. Contrary to these predictions, people routinely consider historic, nonrecoverable costs when making decisions about the future. This behavior is called the *sunk-cost effect*.[3] The sunk-cost effect is an escalation of commitment and has been defined as the "greater tendency to continue an endeavor once an investment in money, time, or effect has been made."[4]

Sunk costs have two important dimensions: size and timing.[5] Consider the following two scenarios.

A family has tickets to a basketball game, which they have been anticipating for some time. The tickets are worth $40. On the day of the game, a big snowstorm hits their area. Although they can still go to the game, the snowstorm will cause a hassle that will reduce the pleasure of watching the game. Is the family more likely to go to the game if they purchased the tickets for $40 or if the tickets were given to them for free?

The common belief is that the family is more likely to go to the game if they purchased the tickets. Note that the $40 cost of the ticket does not factor into the hassle of the snowstorm or the pleasure derived from the game. Yet people consider the sunk cost in their decision whether to go. A family that pays for the tickets opens a mental account. If they do not attend the game, the family is forced to close the mental account without the benefit of the purchase, resulting in a perceived loss. The family wishes to avoid the emotional pain of the loss; therefore, they are more likely to go to the game. Had the tickets been free, the account could be closed without a benefit or a cost.

This example illustrates that the size of the sunk cost is an important factor in decision making. In both cases the family had tickets, but it was the cost of the tickets ($40 versus $0) that mattered. The next example illustrates that the timing of the sunk cost is also an important component.

A family has long anticipated going to the basketball game, which will take place next week. On the day of the game, a snowstorm occurs. Is the family more likely to go to the game if they purchased the $40 tickets one year ago or yesterday?

In both cases, the $40 purchase price is a sunk cost. However, does the timing of the sunk cost matter? Yes, the family is more likely to go to the game if they purchased the tickets yesterday than if they purchased the tickets last year. The pain of closing a mental account without a benefit decreases with time. In short, the negative impact of a sunk cost depreciates over time.

ECONOMIC IMPACT

The previous examples demonstrate that people are willing to incur monetary costs to facilitate their mental budgeting process. Remember that people tend to prepay for some purchases, and they prefer to get paid *after* doing work. By accelerating payments and delaying income, they are not taking advantage of the time value of money principles. Traditional economic theories predict that people would prefer the opposite: delaying payment and accelerating income to maximize the present value of their wealth.

Mental accounting causes people to want to match the emotional costs and benefits of a purchase. Their determination frequently leads to expensive decisions. Consider the following example.[6]

Fifty-six MBA students were asked to select a loan to finance the $7,000 cost of a home-remodeling project. The project involved redecorating (new carpet, wallpaper, paint, and so on) and would last four years, at which point they would have to redecorate again. Two borrowing options were given. One loan had a three-year term and an interest rate of 12 percent. The other was a 15-year loan with an 11 percent interest rate. Both loans could be prepaid without penalty.

Note that the long-term loan has a lower interest rate. In addition, the 15-year loan can be converted into a 3-year loan (that has a lower interest rate) by merely accelerating the payments. That is, you could calculate the monthly payment needed to pay off the 15-year loan in only 3 years. Because the interest rate on the 15-year loan is lower than on the 3-year loan, the monthly payments would be lower. When asked, 74 percent of the MBA students preferred the three-year loan. These students indicated a willingness to incur monetary costs (in the form of a higher interest rate) to make it easier to integrate related costs and benefits. The students were willing to pay a higher interest rate in order to guarantee that the loan will be paid in only three years. This is an example of the self-control problem discussed in Chapter 11.

Another interesting example involves the well-known problem that people face self-control challenges while saving money out of their paycheck. People are much more likely to save or invest money from a windfall than from regular income. This effect has been shown in windfalls like annual bonuses and tax refunds. Economists have traditionally argued that overpaying withholding tax every paycheck and then receiving a large tax refund is like giving the government an interest-free loan. However, many people like doing this because it causes a large windfall every year that they can save (at least partially).

Saving an equivalent amount every paycheck is just too difficult. This is because people consider windfalls to be in their "wealth" mental account and paycheck income to be in their "consumption" mental account. It is hard for people to save (a wealth account) from a consumption mental account.

U.S. President Obama signed the Recovery Act stimulus bill on February 17, 2009. The bill was intended to stimulate an economy struggling with recession. One aspect of that bill was to reduce the tax withholding rates employers use to withhold employees' income taxes. This change caused most people to see a small increase in their paycheck because fewer taxes were taken out. The overall income marginal tax rates were not changed, so the total amount of income taxes a person would owe did not change. Thus, this reduction in withholding simply allowed people to spend a little more each month (which would hopefully improve the economy), but that was offset by a smaller refund than expected the following year.

Could this change have an impact on people's wealth? Would this cause people to save less the following year when they receive a lower tax refund than usual? Naomi Feldman conducted an analysis of a similar change in the withholding tables directed by President George H. W. Bush in 1992.[7] She studied the saving contributions to an Individual Retirement Account (IRA). She found that every $100 of taxes that were shifted from a refund to paychecks reduced the likelihood of IRA savings by 19.7 percent. The average shift in tax payments in 1992 was a $24.42 monthly paycheck increase and a $293 reduction in the 1993 tax refund. These results represent an average 57.6 percent decrease in the IRA participation rate. This effect is also likely to be true for the 2009 change in withholding and the subsequent 2010 IRA participation rate. Because of mental accounting, the Recovery Act will likely decrease people's savings and thus lower their level of wealth.

MENTAL ACCOUNTING AND INVESTING

Consider how mental accounting and loss aversion impact the behavior of taxi cabdrivers in New York. First, they evaluate every day separately (mental accounting) on how much money they made compared to some reference point. Because they are loss averse, they work very hard on bad days to earn the reference amount to avoid that day being a loss. As a result, cabdrivers work longer hours during bad days and fewer hours during good days.[8] This is an inefficient work schedule. The mental accounting process causes them to view their work time too narrowly. The cabdriver could work fewer total hours and make more money for the week by working longer hours during good days and cutting the bad days short.

Investor Trading

Just as taxi drivers view each day separately, investors view each investment separately. Decision makers tend to place each investment into a separate mental account. Each investment is treated individually, and interactions are overlooked. This mental process can adversely affect an investor's wealth in several ways. First, mental accounting exacerbates the disposition effect discussed in Chapter 3. Recall that investors avoid selling stocks with losses because they do not want to experience the emotional pain of regret. Selling the losing stock closes the mental account, triggering regret.

Consider the wealth-maximizing strategy of conducting a *tax swap*.[9] A tax swap occurs when an investor sells a stock with losses and purchases a similar stock. For example, suppose you own Delta Airlines stock, which has experienced a price decline along with the stocks of the entire airline industry. You could sell the Delta stock and purchase United Airlines stock. This tax swap allows you to capture the capital loss of Delta stock to reduce your taxes while staying invested and waiting for the airline industry rebound.

Why isn't the tax swap strategy used more often? Investors tend to consider the selling of the loser stock as a closing of that mental account and the buying of the similar stock as an opening of a new mental account. This causes two outcomes that affect investors. First, the interaction between these two accounts increases the investor's wealth. Second, the closing of the loser account causes regret. Investors tend to ignore the interaction between accounts; therefore, investors act to avoid regret instead of to maximize wealth.

Mental budgeting compounds the aversion to selling losers. Consider how people value the timing of payments and benefits. As time passes, the purchase of the stock becomes a sunk cost. The emotional pain of wasting some of the sunk cost on a loser diminishes over time.[10] It may be less emotionally distressing for the investor to sell the losing stock later as opposed to earlier.

When investors do decide to sell a loser, they can bundle more than one sale on the same day. Investors can integrate the sale of losers to aggregate the losses and limit the feeling of regret to one time period. In other words, people may combine the separate mental accounts in losing positions and close them out all at once in order to minimize their regret. Instead of using the narrow frame of individual investments, they are able to broaden the frame to several investments. Alternatively, investors like to separate the sale of winners over several days to prolong the more favorable feeling. Sonya Lim studied the selling behavior of 50,000 brokerage accounts (425,000 sell trades) from 1991 to 1996.[11] She found that investors are likely to sell more than one losing stock on the same day. On the other hand, if a winner stock is sold, selling another winner stock on the same day is less likely. She concludes, "Investors can maximize their happiness by savoring gains one by one, while minimizing the pain by thinking about the overall loss rather than individual losses." Can the sale with loss be integrated with the sale with a gain at the same time to mitigate the regret? It depends on the relative magnitudes of the loss and gain. Remember that prospect theory (from Chapter 1) states that the pain of a loss is greater than the happiness of a gain of the same magnitude. So, if the magnitude of the loss is larger than the magnitude of the gain, investors will segregate them by selling on different days. If the magnitude of the loss is smaller than the gain, then the investor may integrate them by selling on the same day.

In a follow-up study, Sonya Lim and Alok Kumar investigated whether those investors who can think of their investments in a broader frame suffer less from other behavioral problems.[12] Specifically, a narrow framing viewpoint may exacerbate the disposition effect and also cause poor diversification. Clustering trades indicates a broader frame. They find that investors exhibiting a broader frame also exhibit weaker disposition effects and hold better-diversified portfolios.

Asset Allocation

The narrow framing aspect of mental accounting might also explain why so many people do not invest in the stock market,[13] even though stocks have a high mean return. The stock market risk has nearly zero correlation with a person's other economic risk, namely, labor income risk and housing price risk. Therefore, adding even a small amount of stock market risk provides diversification of one's overall economic risk. However, in isolation, which is how people tend to view things, the stock market appears much riskier than labor income risk and housing price risk.

As an example, consider the distribution of asset allocation within 401(k) retirement plans. A study of nearly 7,000 accounts from one large firm found the allocations to be strongly bimodal.[14] Figure 6.1 shows that about 48 percent of the participants do not allocate any money to equities. Another 22 percent allocate all of their money to equities. In all, 70 percent of the accounts were completely undiversified among asset classes. These allocations seem more consistent with mental accounting than with decision making from a portfolio perspective.

Also, mental accounting tends to cause investors to make decisions about one of their investment accounts without considering their other accounts. That is, instead of creating a total asset allocation of their complete portfolio, they consider each account separately. By narrowly framing each account, they may find that the total asset allocation becomes unattractive. Consider that the typical

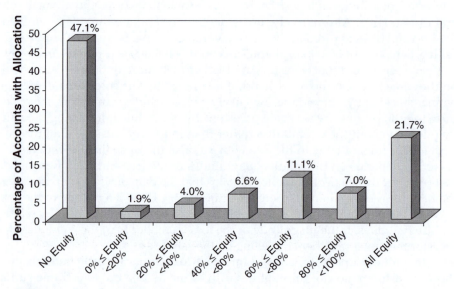

FIGURE 6.1 Retirement Plan Allocation to Equities

401(k) plan has employees make allocation decisions for their own contribution. But the asset allocation of the matching contribution by the firm is usually made by the firm, not the employee. Does the employee consider the predetermined allocation of the matching contribution when deciding the allocation of their own contribution? Analysis of one firm's change in their 401(k) plan illustrates that employees do not take into account the matching allocation.[15] Before the policy change, employees chose only their own contribution's allocation. The matching contribution was entirely in employer stock. After the change in March of 2003, the employees chose the asset allocation for both their own and the matching contributions.

Figure 6.2 shows the contributions to employer stock. During the six months before this policy change, new employees decided only the allocation of their own contributions. They selected an average 25 percent of their own contributions to employer stock, while the match was entirely of employer stock. Thus, the total retirement plan allocation, both their own and the matching contributions, was nearly 60 percent in employer stock. During the six months after the policy change, new employees allocated about 25 percent of their own contributions and about one-third of the matching contribution to employer stock. This allocation made the total retirement plan allocation to employer stock about 27 percent. Notice that this is less than half of the allocation made in the pre-change period. If participants wanted only 27 percent of their total assets allocated to employer stock, then they should have allocated none of their

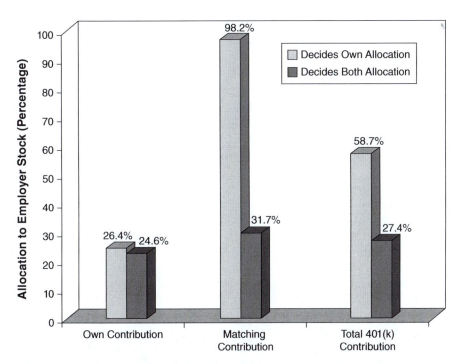

FIGURE 6.2 Allocation to Employer Stock When Employees Decide

contributions to employer stock when the match was pre-determined into employer stock. Yet, the allocation of their own contributions was almost the same between the two periods. The allocation of the matching account did not seem to impact their allocations in their own accounts!

Mental accounting also affects investors' perceptions of portfolio risks. The tendency to overlook the interaction between investments causes investors to misperceive the risk of adding a security to an existing portfolio. Chapter 7 describes how mental accounting leads to the building of portfolios layer by layer. Each layer represents the investment choices that satisfy various mental accounts. This process allows investors to meet the goals of each mental account separately. It does not lead to the benefits of diversification shown by portfolio theory. In fact, people usually don't think in terms of portfolio risk. Consider a financial advisor advising his or her clients that they should take a little more investment risk to acquire more money for retirement. If asked, would you prefer to take a *lot* more risk with *some* of your money, or would you prefer to take a *little* more risk with *all* of your money?[16] People tend to think in terms of the first choice, which is consistent with mental accounting. The second choice is from the perspective of modern portfolio theory.

Market Impact

Mental accounting sets the foundation for segregating different investments in separate accounts, each to be considered alone. A reference point in each mental account determines whether the current position is considered a gain or a loss. This mental accounting then allows for the application of other psychological biases, like the disposition effect (see Chapter 3). Remember that the disposition effect influences investors to sell winners quickly and hold on to losers. Can this combination of mental accounting and disposition effect behavior of individual investors somehow impact stock prices?

If many investors have unrealized capital gains and unrealized capital losses in the same stocks, then their biased trading may distort the stock prices of those firms. Mark Grinblatt and Bing Han argued that a stock that has had good news in the past and increased in price will also have excess selling pressure because of the disposition to sell winners.[17] This selling keeps the winner stock price below fundamental value. Alternatively, a stock with prior adverse news experiences a price decline. However, disposition investors hold losers and this lack of selling keeps the stock price above its fundamental value. They conclude, "In equilibrium, past winners tend to be undervalued and past losers tend to be overvalued" (p. 314). If past winners are undervalued, then they are likely to continue to perform well in the future. Overvalued losers should continue to perform poorly. This pattern is known as stock return *momentum*. Grinblatt and Han claim that the momentum pattern is caused by investors suffering from mental accounting and the disposition account. To illustrate this point, they estimated the amount of unrealized capital gains (and losses) in each stock with a procedure that combines past prices and volume to compute an aggregate cost basis. This cost basis is the reference point used to determine the unrealized capital gain or loss status. Stocks with high estimated unrealized gains outperform stocks with high unrealized losses by 10 percent per year. After controlling for unrealized capital gains and losses, past returns no longer predict future returns. They suggest that what has been known as momentum in returns is really a ramification of mental accounting and the disposition effect. Stocks with paper capital gains will have higher average returns in the future than stocks with paper losses.

Summary

The process of mental accounting leads people to think about each of their investments in isolation. Therefore, people do not think about any benefits or costs associated with the interaction between investments, like diversification and tax swaps. This narrow framing leads to poor asset allocation and too much allocation into an employer's stock. Mental accounting exacerbates the disposition effect. When this is pervasive in society, past winners can be undervalued and past losers can be overvalued, leading to a momentum pattern in the market.

Questions

1. Why do people save money in advance for a vacation but tend to finance a consumer purchase and pay later? What are the factors involved?
2. Why do investors tend to sell losing positions together, on the same day, and separate the sale of winning positions over several days?
3. How does the use of a tax swap overcome some psychological biases?
4. How can changes in tax withholding rates impact people's wealth?
5. Explain how mental accounting combines with the disposition effect to impact stock prices.

Notes

1. Richard Thaler, "Mental Accounting and Consumer Choice," *Marketing Science* 4(1985): 199–214. See also Richard Thaler, "Mental Accounting Matters," *Journal of Behavioral Decision Making* 12(1999): 183–206.
2. Drazen Prelec and George Loewenstein, "The Red and the Black: Mental Accounting of Savings and Debt," *Marketing Science* 17(1998): 4–28.
3. Richard Thaler, "Toward a Positive Theory of Consumer Choice," *Journal of Economics Behavior and Organization* 1(March 1980): 39–60.
4. From Hal Arkes and Catherine Blumer, "The Psychology of Sunk Cost," *Organizational Behavior and Human Decision Processes* 35(February 1985): 124–140.
5. This discussion is adapted from John Gourville and Dilip Soman, "Payment Depreciation: The Behavioral Effects of Temporally Separating Payments from Consumption," *Journal of Consumer Research* 25(1998): 160–174.
6. Eric Hirst, Edward Joyce, and Michael Schadewald, "Mental Accounting and Outcome Contiguity in Consumer-Borrowing Decisions," *Organizational Behavior and Human Decision Processes* 58(1994): 136–152.
7. See Naomi E. Feldman, "Mental Accounting Effects of Income Tax Shifting," *Review of Economics and Statistics* 92(2010): 70–86.
8. Colin Camerer, Linda Babcock, George Loewenstein, and Richard Thaler, "Labor supply of New York City cabdrivers: One day at a time," *Quarterly Journal of Economics* 112(1997): 407–441.

9. This discussion is adapted from Hersh Shefrin and Meir Statman, "The Disposition to Sell Winners Too Early and Ride Losers Too Long: Theory and Evidence," *Journal of Finance* 40(1984): 777–790.

10. John Gourville and Dilip Soman, "Payment Depreciation: The Behavioral Effects of Temporally Separating Payments from Consumption," *Journal of Consumer Research* 25(1998): 160–174.

11. Sonya Seongyeon Lim, "Do Investors Integrate Losses and Segregate Gains? Mental Accounting and Investor Trading Decisions," *Journal of Business* 79(2006): 2539–2573.

12. Alok Kumar and Sonya Seongyeon Lim, "How Do Decision Frames Influence the Stock Investment Choices of Individual Investors?" *Management Science* 54(2008): 1052–1064.

13. Nicholas Barberis, Ming Huang, and Richard Thaler, "Individual Preferences, Monetary Gambles, and Stock Market Participation: A Case for Narrow Framing," *American Economic Review* 96(2006): 1069–1090.

14. Julie Agnew, Pierluigi Balduzzi, and Annika Sundén, "Portfolio Choice and Trading in a Large 401(k) Plan," *American Economic Review* 93(2003): 193–215.

15. James Choi, David Laibson, and Brigitte Madrian, "Mental Accounting in Portfolio Choice: Evidence from a Flypaper Effect," *American Economic* 99(2009): 2085–2095.

16. Meir Statman, "The Diversification Puzzle," *Financial Analysts Journal* 60(2004): 44–53.

17. Mark Grinblatt and Bing Han, "Prospect Theory, Mental Accounting, and Momentum," *Journal of Financial Economics* 78(2005): 311–339.

Forming Portfolios

Chapter 6 detailed how mental accounting is used to track the costs and benefits associated with each decision. Mental accounting also affects how you view your investment portfolios.

MODERN PORTFOLIO THEORY

Fifty years ago, Nobel Prize–winning economist Harry Markowitz taught us to consider all our investments as one whole portfolio. According to Markowitz, an investor should consider owning the investments that combine to form a portfolio that offers the highest expected return for the level of risk desired. Combining investments into a portfolio requires the investor to think in terms of diversification. Investors like the idea of diversification. However, they implement diversification differently than Markowitz's portfolio theory suggests.

To implement portfolio theory, you must consider three important characteristics of each potential investment. The first two parameters are the expected return and the level of risk (as measured by standard deviation of returns) of the investments. Examining the risk and return makes sense to investors. The third important characteristic is the correlation between the returns of each investment. Correlation is how each investment interacts with the others. Mental accounting makes it difficult to implement this important characteristic.

MENTAL ACCOUNTING AND PORTFOLIOS

Investors typically place each investment into a separate mental account. One outcome of mental accounting is that you discount the interaction between mental accounts, which affects the construction of your portfolio. Consider the high

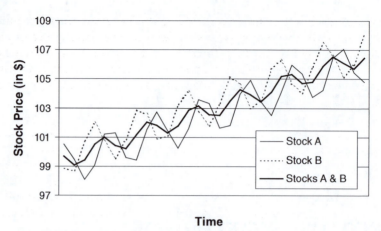

FIGURE 7.1 Combining Stocks into a Portfolio

volatility of the recent stock market. Stocks often experience large price gains and losses each day. Modern portfolio theory shows that different investments can be combined to reduce this volatility. By comparing how the price of different investments changes over time, a lower-risk portfolio can be constructed.

For example, stocks A and B in Figure 7.1 have approximately the same return and variation in stock price over time. Both stocks experience large price changes. However, notice that when stock A is advancing, stock B is often declining. Because stocks A and B frequently move in opposite directions, buying both stocks creates a portfolio with reduced risk. That is, the value of your portfolio varies less over time when you own stocks A and B than it would if you owned only one of those stocks.

However, creating a portfolio that reduces risk (in the modern portfolio theory sense) means considering the interaction between different investments. Unfortunately, investors often treat each investment as a different mental account and tend to ignore the interaction between those mental accounts. Therefore, the most useful tool in constructing portfolios and reducing risk, the correlation between investments, is difficult to utilize because of mental accounting.[1]

Instead, portfolios are built by making buying decisions on each investment individually. In general, investors tend to pick investments as if they were picking food at a buffet: "This looks interesting . . . I think I'll have some of that . . . maybe a little of this one. . . . I've heard about that one. . . ." The decision to purchase a new security and open a new mental account does not include the investment's correlation with other investments because the mental accounts do not interact with each other.

PERCEPTIONS ON RISK

Viewing each investment as a separate mental account causes investors to misperceive risk. Investors evaluate each potential investment as if it were the only investment they will own. However, most investors already have a portfolio and are considering other investments to add to it. Therefore, the most important consideration for the evaluation is how the expected risk and return of the portfolio will change when a new investment is added. In other words, it is how the new investment interacts with the existing portfolio that matters. Unfortunately, people have trouble evaluating the interactions between mental accounts. Consider the following problem:

You have a diversified portfolio of large domestic and international stocks with some fixed-income securities. You are examining the following investments: commodities, corporate bonds (high grade), emerging markets stocks, European and East Asian stocks, high-yield bonds, real estate, Russell 2000 Growth Index, small capitalization stocks, and treasury bills. How does the addition of each investment change the risk of the existing portfolio?

I asked 45 undergraduate and 27 graduate students taking the investments course and 16 investment club participants to sort these nine investments by their level of risk contribution to the portfolio. Note that the experiment participants were not given return, risk, or correlation information. They had to make decisions based on their own knowledge and information. Figure 7.2 reports the results of the three groups.

Treasury bills and corporate bonds are viewed as adding the least risk, whereas real estate, commodities, and high-yield bonds add higher risk. Small capitalization stocks and foreign stocks add the most risk to the portfolio. Notice that all three groups provide a similar ranking of how each investment contributes risk to the existing portfolio. The last ranking in the figure was calculated

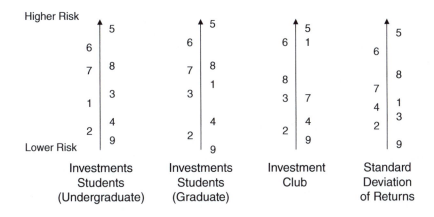

1. Commodities (gold, oil, etc.) 2. Corporate Bonds 3. High-Yield Corporate Bonds 4. Real Estate 5. Stocks from Emerging Market Countries 6. Stocks from Europe and East Asia 7. Small Capitalization Stocks 8. Small Capitalization Growth Stocks 9. Treasury Bills

FIGURE 7.2 Investor's View of Risk Contribution to Portfolio

using the investments' standard deviation of monthly returns during 1980–1997.[2] Standard deviation is a good measure of an investment's risk. The rank order and magnitude of risk contribution of the three different groups is similar to the risk ranking using standard deviation as the measure.

However, standard deviation measures the riskiness of the investment, not how the risk of the portfolio would change if the investment were added. Remember the earlier example where stocks A and B had the same risk but combined to reduce risk in a portfolio? It is not the level of risk for each investment that is important; the important measure is how each investment interacts with the existing portfolio. Consider Figure 7.3A.

Panel A of the figure plots the standard deviation of monthly stock returns for each investment versus the investment's contribution of risk to the existing portfolio, as measured by beta. A beta of greater than 1 indicates that the investment would increase the risk of the portfolio. A beta smaller than 1 indicates that adding the security would reduce the risk of the portfolio.

Notice that the last risk ranking in Figure 7.2 is simply the y-axis of Figure 7.3A. Because of mental accounting, investors view the risk of adding an investment to their portfolio as the individual risk (standard deviation) of the investment. However, the real contribution to portfolio risk of the investment is measured on the x-axis. Figure 7.3B shows just the x-axis—the interaction between the investment and the existing portfolio.

Panel B shows that if you want to reduce the risk of your portfolio, you should add real estate and commodities. Does this come as a surprise? Small capitalization stocks and Russell 2000 Growth Index–type stocks increase the risk of the portfolio. Viewed by themselves, emerging markets stocks are the most risky investments in the example. However, they would interact with the existing portfolio such that they would reduce the risk of the portfolio, if they were added.

Risk Perception in the Real World

Public pension systems demonstrate how the misperception of risk from mental accounting affects portfolios. Public pension systems are the retirement plans of public employees such as teachers, police, and state and city workers. The state or local government sets aside money each year to be invested and ultimately used as the employees' retirement income. Professional money managers are hired to invest the money, but the government may restrict the managers from investing in specific securities in an attempt to limit the risk of the portfolio. Because of mental accounting, the government officials tend to use each security's individual risk (as in Figure 7.3A) instead of the interaction risk effect (as in Figure 7.3B) to make these decisions.

The Government Finance Officers Association surveyed public pension plans in 1999. The plan managers were asked about the investment restrictions under which they operate. A total of 211 retirement plan managers responded.[3] Remember that Figure 7.3B showed that real estate, corporate bonds, and even foreign stocks can reduce the risk of a typical portfolio. However, 14 plan managers responded that they could not invest in real estate. A total of

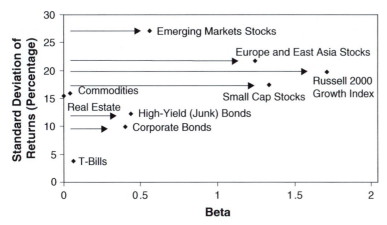

FIGURE 7.3A   Investment Risk and Risk Contribution to Portfolio

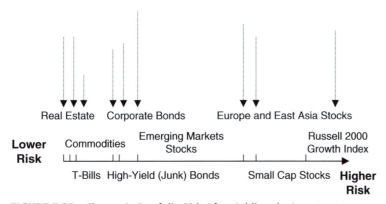

FIGURE 7.3B   Change in Portfolio Risk After Adding the Investment

8 plan managers could not invest in corporate bonds, and 19 plan managers could not invest in foreign securities. Many more plans had other limitations, such as a maximum investment in real estate, corporate bonds, and foreign securities of no more than 5 percent of the portfolio. Interestingly, three plan managers could not invest in U.S. stocks at all. Those government policymakers need to read this book!

BUILDING BEHAVIORAL PORTFOLIOS

Investors like the idea of diversification, but they don't build portfolios in the manner suggested by portfolio theory. How, then, do investors build a diversified portfolio?

Hersh Shefrin and Meir Statman show how the psychological tendencies of investors cause them to think of their portfolios as a pyramid of assets.[4] Each layer in the pyramid represents assets intended to meet a particular goal. Consider the pyramid depicted in Figure 7.4.

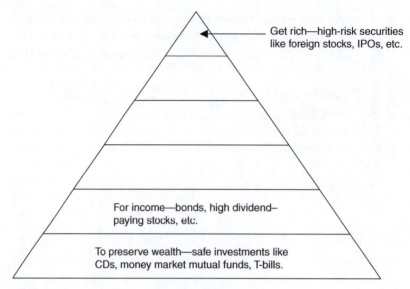

FIGURE 7.4 Pyramid Depicting Behavioral Portfolio

People have separate mental accounts for each investment goal, and the investor is willing to take different levels of risk for each goal. Investments are selected for each mental account by finding assets that match the expected risk and return of the mental account.

First, investors have a goal of safety. Therefore, they allocate enough assets in the safest layer (the bottom of the pyramid), as required by their mental accounts. Then mental accounts with higher levels of expected return and risk tolerance allocate assets to appropriate investments in another layer. For example, retired investors need investment income. The income goal is met in a layer of the pyramid with assets invested in bonds and stocks that pay high dividends. After the income goal is met, the retiree's next goal might be to keep up with inflation. This investor would then have a set of assets in a layer that invests for growth.

Each mental account has an amount of money designated for that particular goal. It is the number of mental accounts requiring safety that determines the amount of money placed in safe investments. In contrast, some mental accounts designate "get-rich" assets. In sum, the total asset allocation of an investor's portfolio is determined by how much money is designated for each asset class by the mental accounts. Investors without many safety-oriented goals will place greater amounts of money in high-risk securities. Investors who have stronger safety or income goals will have more securities in those layers of the pyramid.

Consider the average investor. The average investor has assets in a 401(k) pension plan that seems well diversified to the employee (but see the next two sections). Because the 401(k) plan matches the retirement income goals of the person, the next level of the pyramid might be to achieve a higher standard of living in retirement or to save for a child's college education. Mutual fund investments fit this goal nicely.

Higher up the pyramid, a person may want to become rich. A discount brokerage account can be used to try to meet this goal. The median number of stocks owned in a brokerage account is only three,[5] and the median investor trades about three times per year. This low level of diversification might be a problem if it represents a significant portion of the investor's wealth. In addition, investors may sometimes use the stock market to gamble. Alok Kumar identifies stocks with lottery features and finds that people who have a propensity to gamble are also more likely to buy these stocks.[6] Just like the lottery, these lottery-type stocks underperform, but provide a small chance for a big profit.

The result of these various goals and mental accounts is that the average investor ends up with a variety of miniportfolios. The makeup of the overall portfolio is determined, formed, and changed because of the distribution of investment goals and associated mental accounts. Investors tend to overlook the interaction among mental accounts and among investment assets. As a result, investor diversification comes from investment goal diversification rather than from a purposeful asset diversification, as described in Markowitz's portfolio theory.

Ultimately, this means that most investors do not have efficient portfolios. As a consequence, investors are taking too much risk for the level of expected return they are getting. Stated another way, investors could obtain higher returns for the level of risk they are taking.

Household Portfolios

Investor behavior has been examined using detailed datasets of brokerage or retirement plan accounts. However, the diversification used by households may be best studied by examining the entire portfolio of household financial assets. Every three years, the Federal Reserve Board conducts the Survey of Consumer Finances (SCF) by interviewing around four thousand households about their financial assets.

Valery Polkovnichenko examined diversification by households using the SCF surveys from 1983 to 2001.[7] He finds many behaviors that are consistent with people having preferences for separating investment assets to align with separate goals. For example, each household exhibits both risk-aversion and risk-seeking behavior at the same time. They invest both in diversified portfolios like mutual funds and in undiversified stock portfolios with few individual stocks. Consider the households with between $100,000 and $1 million in financial asset wealth. Over the years, 10–15 percent of these households own no stocks (either directly or indirectly through funds). Of those households with stock market ownership, the median household has 15 percent of its financial wealth in a stock portfolio consisting of only four stocks! This median household also has 49 percent of its financial wealth in diversified stock portfolios through mutual funds and pension plans.

Note how this behavior is consistent with investing for two different layers of the behavioral pyramid. A diversified equity portfolio is ideal for achieving moderate riches for retirement. It is not appropriate for achieving great riches. After all, we know that we will not earn a 1,000 percent return in a couple of years through a diversified portfolio. Aspirations like this require an investment in an undiversified portfolio or lottery tickets, no matter how unlikely their success. The investment in four stocks is consistent with the desire for a long-shot gamble at getting rich.

Preferred Risk Habitat

People try to match their level of risk aversion to their investments. However, they do not appear to match their preferred risk level to the risk of their total portfolio. Instead, they tend to use their desired risk level to help them pick each of the individual components that make up the portfolio. That is, investors break up the complex portfolio creation decision into simpler subproblems of finding portfolio components. Each component matches the investor's preferred risk level.

Consider this illustration. Say that an investor decides that his level of risk aversion is such that it matches an investment volatility (standard deviation) of 50 percent. His investment opportunity set includes stocks with increasing levels of risk measured as volatilities of 20, 30, 40, 50, 60, 70, and 80 percent. How does he match his investments to his risk level? One possibility is that if he narrowly frames each stock individually, he could allocate half of the portfolio to the lowest risk stock (of 20 percent volatility) and half to the highest risk stock (of 80 percent volatility) and have a portfolio with average volatility of 50 percent the desired level. A second possibility is that he could allocate to the middle volatility stocks (40, 50, and 60 percent) to form the desired average risk level. A third option would be to take the modern portfolio approach and view the stocks from a broader frame. Combining the stocks might create diversification effects that would lower the total portfolio risk. So he could pick the riskier stocks (60, 70, and 80 percent volatility) and create a total portfolio volatility of the desired 50 percent.

Which of these three options describe investor behavior? Dan Dorn and Gur Huberman argue that investors tend to behave like the second option.[8] They select a level of risk and then pick individual stocks, all with that risk profile. By examining over 20,000 clients at a German broker, they find that investors tend to pick a preferred risk habitat and then pick from the stocks in that habitat. When they replace a stock in their portfolio, they buy a new stock that is in the same risk habitat as the one sold. Lastly, they find that those investors who are most prone to specializing in a risk habitat underperform other investors because they take too much diversifiable risk. They would be better off thinking more broadly and designing a diversified portfolio with total risk that matches the risk habitat.

NAÏVE DIVERSIFICATION

Although investors should consider their entire portfolio when making investment decisions, they usually make decisions only within the narrow context of the situation. For example, consider investing for your retirement. Some of your assets will be in retirement plans, such as individual retirement accounts and 401(k) plans, and other assets will not be. Suppose the most efficient portfolio for you includes 50 percent stocks and 50 percent bonds. You probably will put half of your retirement plan money in stocks and half in bonds. You will do the same with the assets outside the retirement plans. However, this is not the best allocation. The reason is that you have to pay taxes on income from assets outside the retirement plans, such as from your bonds.

The better choice would be to invest the money within the retirement plans in bonds and buy the stocks with the assets outside the retirement plans. The overall portfolio would still be a mix of 50 percent stocks and 50 percent bonds, but you would owe less in taxes every year. However, this allocation is hard for investors because the conservative allocation of bonds in the retirement plans does not match their investing goals as indicated by the retirement mental account.

Since many participants in a defined contribution retirement plan are unsure of how to design an appropriate portfolio, a predetermined fund has recently become a popular offering. These funds are called either target-date funds or life-cycle funds. The idea is that the investor can select the appropriate fund to match when he or she plans to retire, say the year 2035. The target date 2035 fund may have a 50 percent allocation to stocks now, but that will decline over time as the retirement date approaches. The fund adjusts to the life-cycle risks of the investor as the investor ages. For participants who do not want to fret over the initial allocation choices and the ongoing rebalancing of the 401(k) plan, this is an ideal option. In most cases, the participant who chooses the life-cycle fund should allocate all of his or her retirement assets to it. Yet, that is not how these funds are being used. In pension plans using Vanguard funds, William Nessmith and Stephen Utkus found that only about half of the people contributing to the target-date fund do so exclusively.[9] The other half of the people often contribute to three, four, or more other choices. Indeed, those investors choosing a life-cycle fund in combination with other funds tend to contribute less than half of their retirement money to it. It is interesting to note that usually investors are underdiversified, but when given a chance to invest in a fully diversified portfolio created with their age in mind, they choose to put only some of their money in it.

Retirement Plans

The 401(k) retirement plan is a good example of investor mental accounting and naïve diversification. Employers offer different investment choices within 401(k) plans. For example, one plan may have one bond fund and three stock funds to choose from, and another plan may have one bond fund and one stock fund. Which investments do employees choose?

Employees have a tendency to diversify their 401(k) investments by using a $1/n$ rule. The old adage says that we should "never put all our eggs in one basket." But the adage doesn't give us any direction on how to distribute our eggs. Should we divide them evenly between baskets? If three 401(k) choices are available, should we allocate one-third to each of the three choices?

Interestingly, this occurs no matter what the choices are. For example, the plan offered to TWA pilots had five stocks funds and one bond fund. If all pilots used the $1/n$ rule, then we would expect 83 percent (5/6) of the average portfolio to be invested in stocks. Indeed, the TWA pilots invested an average of 75 percent in stocks, which was much higher than the 57 percent national average. Alternatively, University of California (UC) employees were offered one stock fund and four bond funds. The average stock holdings for UC employees amounted to only 34 percent. Indeed, the number and type of investment offerings seem to play an important role in the asset allocation of employees. At least some employees appear to use the naïve diversification rule of $1/n$.[10] When many choices are available, employees tend to pick just three or four of them and then allocate their contribution evenly between them.[11]

Two scholars, Guido Baltussen and Gerrit Post, examine people's process for choosing investments within a controlled experiment.[12] They use financially trained subjects and real money, having them pick from three (or four) investment choices with clearly shown risk and return characteristics. They find that a large majority appear to first narrowly frame each potential investment and determine if the risk/return characteristics are acceptable or not. Of the set that are viewed acceptable, most of the subjects divided their money evenly between them. This behavior persisted even when the experiment included a choice that might have looked inferior in isolation, but would have created great diversification benefits if combined with the other choices. Unfortunately, the subjects eliminated that portfolio before allocating their funds. They call this behavior the *conditional 1/n heuristic*. That is, people use the $1/n$ rule conditional on first eliminating some alternatives.

Another example is the mental accounting of company stock in the 401(k) plan. Employees appear to treat the stock of the company they work for as different from other stocks. A 1995 survey by John Hancock Financial Services found that a majority of employees believe their own company stock is safer than a diversified portfolio. Interestingly, years after Enron showed us how risky it is to invest in your employer's stock, more than 50 percent of assets in many large corporate 401(k) plans are still invested in company stock.[13] Indeed, 5 million people have more than 60 percent of their account balance investment in their employer's stock.

Company stock is frequently one of the 401(k) choices for employees. In a study of 170 different corporate 401(k) plans, Shlomo Benartzi and Richard Thaler found that 103 plans include company stock as an option. Of the 67 plans that did not include company stock, employees allocated 49.2 percent of their assets to stocks. This nearly 50–50 split is common. However, employees who have the company stock as an option have an average of 42 percent of their assets in the company stock. If they also want a 50–50 split between stocks and bonds, then they should invest most of the rest of their assets in bonds. However, they do not do this. Instead, they split the rest of their assets 50–50 between stocks and bonds. In this way, employees in plans with company stock end up having an average of 71 percent of their portfolio in stocks. These investors appear to put their company stock into its own mental account that is not associated with other stocks.

Summary

The tools of traditional finance, like modern portfolio theory, can help investors establish efficient portfolios to maximize their wealth with acceptable levels of risk. However, mental accounting makes it difficult to implement these tools. Instead, investors use mental accounting to match different investing goals to different asset allocations. This often leads to investors diversifying their portfolios by goal rather than in total. When investors pick investments in each goal-focused miniportfolio, they examine each choice's individual risk and return characteristics and ignore their diversification characteristics. They eliminate the choices they view as inferior and then often simply divide their money equally among the acceptable choices.

Even investors who overcome their tendency toward mental accounting and implement modern portfolio efficiency in their portfolios often find themselves second-guessing over time. The concept of integrating asset classes that exhibit a low correlation means that one or more asset classes held probably will be performing poorly at any given time. Even investors who believe in the diversification argument find themselves wanting out of the underperforming asset class in their portfolios.

Questions

1. How does mental accounting make the concept of correlation difficult for investors to implement?
2. Consider a family of 40-something parents and teenage children. If the family forms its portfolio through a behavioral process, what might it look like? Compare it with what a portfolio would look like if formed on modern portfolio theory principles.
3. Describe the stocks in an investor's portfolio when he picks from his preferred risk habitat.
   Give specific examples. How is this likely to impact the diversification of the portfolio?
4. How does the number of investment choices tend to affect the allocation in an employee's 401(k) plan?
5. If an investor is choosing among four investment choices (a small firm fund, a SP500 Index fund, a technology stock fund, and a bond fund), how would the final asset allocation differ between using the $1/n$ rule versus the conditional $1/n$ heuristic?

Notes

1. Roger G. Clarke, Scott Krase, and Meir Statman, "Tracking Errors, Regret, and Tactical Asset Allocation," *Journal of Portfolio Management* 20(1994): 16–24.
2. Data for these figures come from table 3.7 (p. 93) of Frank K. Reilly and Keith C. Brown, *Investment Analysis and Portfolio Management* (Fort Worth: Dryden Press, Harcourt College Publishers, 2000).
3. These results are calculated using the Pendat 2000 Database, which can be obtained from the Government Finance Officers Association.
4. Hersh Shefrin and Meir Statman, "Behavioral Portfolio Theory," *Journal of Financial and Quantitative Analysis* 35(2000): 127–151; Meir Statman, "Foreign Stocks in Behavioral Portfolios," *Financial Analysts Journal* (March/April 1999): 12–16.
5. Ravi Dhar and Ning Zhu, "Up Close and Personal: An Individual Level Analysis of the Disposition Effect," *Management Science* 52(2006): 726–740.
6. Alok Kumar, "Who Gambles in the Stock Market?" *Journal of Finance* 64(2009): 1889–1933.

7. Valery Polkovnichenko, "Household Portfolio Diversification: A Case for Rank-Dependent Preferences," *Review of Financial Studies* 18(2005): 1467–1500.

8. Daniel Dorn and Gur Huberman, "Preferred Risk Habitat of Individual Investors," *Journal of Financial Economics* 97(2010): 155–173.

9. William Nessmith and Stephen Utkus, "Target-Date Funds: Plan and Participant Adoption in 2007," *Vanguard Center for Retirement Research* 33(2008): 1–16.

10. This example and others can be found in Shlomo Benartzi and Richard H. Thaler, "Naïve Diversification Strategies in Defined Contribution Savings Plans," *American Economic Review* 91(2001): 79–98.

11. Gur Huberman and Wei Jiang, "Offering Versus Choice in 401(k) Plans: Equity Exposure and Number of Funds," *Journal of Finance* 61(2006): 763–801.

12. Guido Baltussen and Gerrit T. Post, "Irrational Diversification: An Examination of Individual Portfolio Choice," *Journal of Financial and Quantitative Analysis* 46(2011): 1463–1491.

13. Shlomo Benartzi, Richard Thaler, Stephen Utkus, and Cass Sunstein, "The Law and Economics of Company Stock in 401(k) Plans," *Journal of Law and Economics* 50(2007): 45–79.

Representativeness and Familiarity

Psychological research has shown that the brain uses shortcuts to reduce the complexity of analyzing information. Psychologists call these heuristic simplifications. These mental shortcuts allow the brain to generate an estimate of the answer before fully digesting all the available information. Two examples of shortcuts are known as representativeness and familiarity. Using these shortcuts allows the brain to organize and quickly process large amounts of information. However, these shortcuts also make it hard for investors to analyze new information correctly and can lead to inaccurate conclusions.

REPRESENTATIVENESS

The brain makes the assumption that things that share similar qualities are quite alike. Representativeness is judgment based on stereotypes. Consider the following question:

Mary is quiet, studious, and concerned with social issues. While an undergraduate at Berkeley, she majored in English literature and environmental studies. Given this information, indicate which of the following three cases is most probable:

   A. Mary is a librarian.
   B. Mary is a librarian and a member of the Sierra Club.
   C. Mary works in the banking industry.

I have asked this question to undergraduate investment students, MBA graduate students, and financial advisors. In all three groups, more than half of the people choose case B—Mary is a librarian and a member of the Sierra Club. People select this case because being a librarian and a member of the Sierra Club is representative of the type of career a studious person concerned with social issues might pick. However, the question asked which case is more probable, not which case would make Mary the happiest.

Case A—Mary is a librarian—is a superior choice to B. Being a librarian and a Sierra Club member is a subset of being a librarian. Because case A includes case B, it is more probable that case A is true. Usually a quarter to a third of the people asked understand this and choose case A over case B.

However, the best choice is case C—Mary works in the banking industry. Many more people are employed by banks than by libraries. In fact, so many more jobs exist in banking that it is far more probable that someone works in the banking industry than as a librarian. Because working in the banking industry is not "representative" of the shortcut our brains make to describe Mary, few people pick case C.

REPRESENTATIVENESS AND INVESTING

People also make representativeness errors in financial markets. For example, investors confuse a good company with a good investment. Good companies are represented by firms that generate strong earnings, have high sales growth, and have quality management. Or, you may believe a company is good because you like its products or the way it treats its employees. Good investments are stocks that increase in price more than other stocks. Are the stocks of good companies also good investments? The answer might be no.[1]

Classifying good stocks as firms with a history of consistent earnings growth ignores the fact that few companies can sustain the high levels of growth achieved in the past. The popularity of these firms drives prices higher. However, over time it becomes apparent that investors have been too optimistic in predicting future growth, and the stock price falls. This is known as *overreaction*.[2]

Three financial economists examined this issue. Josef Lakonishok, Andrei Shleifer, and Robert Vishny (henceforth LSV) studied the performance of stocks investors typically consider to be growth stocks. These researchers label growth stocks as "glamour" stocks. Stocks of firms that investors typically consider to be bad firms with minimal growth prospects are labeled "value" stocks. Investors consider growth firms to be firms with growing business operations. LSV calculated the average growth rate in sales for all firms over the past five years. The 10 percent of firms with the highest average growth rates were glamour firms, whereas the firms with the lowest sales growth were value firms. Glamour or value—which stocks will be better investments over the next year? The next five years?

Using data for all stocks on the New York Stock Exchange and American Stock Exchange over the period 1963–1990, LSV reported the results in Figure 8.1.[3] If you bought the glamour stocks, you earned an 11.4 percent return the following year. This compares with a return of 18.7 percent for the

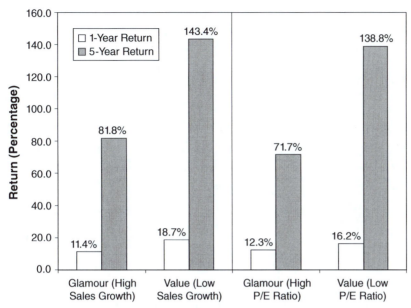

FIGURE 8.1   One-Year and Five-Year Returns for Glamour and Value Stocks

value stocks. The average total return over a five-year period is 81.8 percent for the glamour stocks and 143.4 percent for the value stocks.

Another popular measure of glamour/value stocks is the *price/earnings (P/E) ratio*. Companies with high P/E ratios are more glamorous than firms with low P/E ratios. The figure also demonstrates that value stocks outperform glamour stocks using the P/E ratio measure.

Good companies do not always make good investments. Investors often erroneously believe that the past operating performance of the firm is representative of the future performance, and they ignore information that does not fit this notion. Good companies do not perform well forever, just as bad companies do not perform poorly forever.

Extrapolation Bias

Investors also tend to extrapolate past stock returns into the future. Extrapolation bias is considered to be a subset of the representativeness bias because investors believe that past returns represent what they should expect in the future. Consider the case of whether to be invested in the stock market or not. When do investors get out of the market, and when do they get back in? Figure 8.2 shows flows into (or out of) stock mutual funds every month and the level of the stock market via the S&P (Standard and Poor's) 500 Index. Note how investors were plowing tens of billions of dollars into the stock market each month during the peak of stock market tech bubble in late 1990s and early 2000s. These investors bought high. Then they started to get out of the market in late 2002 and early 2003, right at the bottom. These investors sold low. Also notice the selling at the 2008 and 2009 stock market valley. By the time investors can identify a clear

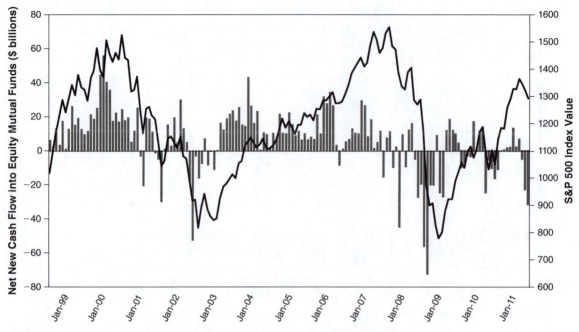

FIGURE 8.2   The Monthly Net Flow into Equity Mutual Funds Versus the S&P 500 Index

trend of the past in order to extrapolate it into the future, they have missed most of the move. Unfortunately, this bias leads investors to buying high and selling low, not a winning investment strategy!

Mary Bange investigates this behavior by studying the weekly and monthly surveys conducted by the American Association of Individual Investors (AAII).[4] AAII surveys its membership regarding their opinion about the stock market and their asset allocation. She finds that when AAII members express a change in their sentiment about the market, their subsequent allocation to stocks also changes. In other words, when investors become more bullish, they follow through and buy more stocks. Does this increase in bullishness come from superior market-timing abilities? No, she finds their market timing to be poor. The reason for their change in sentiment appears to come from past returns on the market. When the stock market had done unusually well during the past three years, investors become more bullish. When the market does poorly, they become more bearish. This extrapolation bias leads to poor asset-allocation timing decisions.

Investors also extrapolate past returns for individual stocks and mutual funds. The good (or bad) performance is expected to continue. For example, a stock that has performed badly for the past three to five years is considered a loser. On the other hand, stocks that have done great for the past three to five years are considered winners. Investors assume this past return is representative of what they can expect in the future. Investors like to chase winners and buy stocks of firms that have trended upward in price.[5] However, losers tend to outperform winners over the next three years by 30 percent.[6] Mutual fund investors also use this same extrapolating heuristic. The mutual funds listed in magazines and newspapers with the highest recent performance receive a flood of new investors. These investors are chasing the winners. Indeed, a study of investor mutual fund trades finds that the investors who are mutual fund trend following are investors who exhibit other behavioral biases in their investment activities.[7] As this is not an optimal strategy, the return chasing money is often referred to as "dumb money."

Indeed, this type of investing is so popular that it has its own name: *momentum investing*. Momentum investors look for stocks and mutual funds that have performed well over the past week, month, or quarter. Momentum traders look for good performers over the past few hours or even minutes. The media exacerbate the bias. For example, every day, the *Wall Street Journal* reports yesterday's biggest percentage gainers, and throughout the day, you can find which stocks have the highest price change for the day at any financial Web site.

Even finance professors are influenced by the representativeness bias. Ivo Welch has implemented several surveys of financial economics professors.[8] The first series of surveys was implemented in 1997 through 1998, and an additional survey was conducted in 1999. These surveys elicited 226 responses. Note that these surveys were completed during a strong bull market. One question asked about the expected annual equity risk premium over the next 30 years. The mean response was 8.2 percent. In a separate question about stock market return mean reversion versus the random walk, the professors tended to lean toward the belief that the stock market mean reverts. Welch again surveyed the profession in 2001, when the market environment was quite different. The S&P 500 Index had declined by approximately 25 percent from its peak. Given the earlier expression that stock returns might exhibit mean reversion, we might expect respondents to express a higher equity premium estimate after a market decline. However, the mean annual 30-year equity risk premium was only 5.5 percent. Note that this is considerably lower than estimates provided only three years earlier. Although their updated estimates were about 2.7 percent lower, they reiterated their belief that stock returns are mean reverting. Yet their estimates are not consistent with that belief. The responses are consistent with the notion that the most recent past is representative of what will happen in the future.

In short, investors interpret the past business operations of a firm and the past performance of stock as representative of future expectations. Unfortunately, firms tend to revert to the mean over the long term. That is, fast-growing firms find that competition increases and slows their rate of growth. Disappointed investors, in turn, find that the stock does not perform as expected.

FAMILIARITY

People prefer things that are familiar to them. Fans root for the local sports teams, and employees like to own their company's stock. This is because the sports teams and the company are familiar to them.

When people are faced with two risky choices and they know more about one than the other, they will pick the more familiar option. Given two different gambles in which the odds of winning are the same but they have more experience with one over the other, people pick the better-known gamble. In fact, they will sometimes pick the more familiar gamble even if the odds of winning are lower.[9]

FAMILIARITY BREEDS INVESTMENT

Tens of thousands of potential stock and bond investments exist in the United States with as many choices overseas as well. So how do investors choose? Do we analyze the expected return and risk of each investment? No, investors trade in the securities with which they are familiar.[10] There is comfort in having your money invested in a business that is visible to you.

As an example, consider the breakup of AT&T. In 1984, the government broke up AT&T's local phone service monopoly into seven regional phone companies known as the "Baby Bells." Twelve years after the breakup, Gur Huberman investigated the ownership of these Baby Bells. He found that investors are more likely to own shares in their local phone company than the phone company of another region; that is, they are more comfortable investing in the more familiar firm. In a similar study of owning utility stocks, investors are found to be four times more likely to own the local utility firm compared to all other utility firms. This preference for the familiar is not reduced in samples of more affluent and sophisticated individual investors.[11] This preference for investing close to home also applies to investment managers.[12]

The inclination to invest in the familiar causes people to invest far more money within their own country than traditional ideas of diversification would suggest. Investors have a "home bias" because companies from their own country are more familiar to them than foreign companies.

Figure 8.3 illustrates the home bias. The stock market in the United States represents over 43 percent of the value of all stocks worldwide. The stock markets in Japan and the United Kingdom represent 10 percent and 7 percent of the worldwide stock market, respectively. Therefore, to fully diversify a stock portfolio, investors should allocate 43 percent of their portfolio to U.S. stocks, 10 percent to Japanese stocks, and 7 percent to U.K. stocks. In fact, traditional portfolio theory suggests that all investors should have this allocation.

When people do invest some of their money in foreign firms, what types of foreign firms do they buy? They buy foreign firms that are familiar, which means large firms with recognizable products. For example, non-Japanese investors tend to own the large Japanese companies.[13] The smaller Japanese firms that attract non-Japanese investors are the ones that have high levels of exports. Figure 8.3 shows that German mutual funds invest a relatively smaller amount in their domestic equity. When they invest in foreign equity, where do they invest? Figure 8.4 shows the six countries with the highest allocations of German mutual funds.[14] Note that their foreign investments do not follow the proportion of worldwide equity. They invest nearly 13 percent in the United States, which has 43 percent of the world's equity. But Germans invest almost as much in France, which has only 5 percent of the world's equity. This overinvesting in some countries and underinvesting in others is called the *foreign bias*. Germans tend to overinvest in countries that are geographically close or have similar

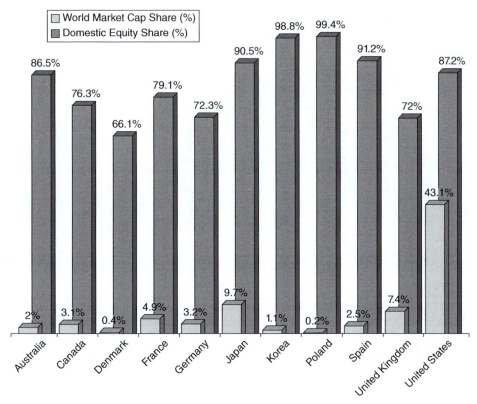

FIGURE 8.3 Market Weight of Country's Stock Market Compared to Total World (foreground) Percentage Share of Domestic Equity in the Country's Equity Portfolio (background)

culture. Countries that seem distant (both geographically and culturally), like Japan for German investors, receive underinvestments.

Chapter 7 illustrated that people do not think of their portfolios from a modern portfolio theory (MPT) perspective. If investors did use MPT when forming their portfolios, they probably would own far more foreign equities. Indeed, the small allocation that investors place in foreign equities implies that they perceive the riskiness of foreign assets to be two to five times larger than they historically have been.[15] Investors also perceive the return of familiar assets to be higher than those of unfamiliar assets.

Merrill Lynch surveys fund managers from around the world every month. Managers from continental Europe predict that their domestic stock returns will be higher than those of the United Kingdom, the United States, and Japan.[16] At the same time, managers in the United Kingdom predict that their domestic returns will be the highest. In short, investors are more bullish on their domestic market relative to foreign markets. The familiarity bias causes investors to be too confident in stocks that are familiar, judging them too optimistically on expected return and risk. Likewise, the stocks that are unfamiliar are judged too pessimistically on risk and return.

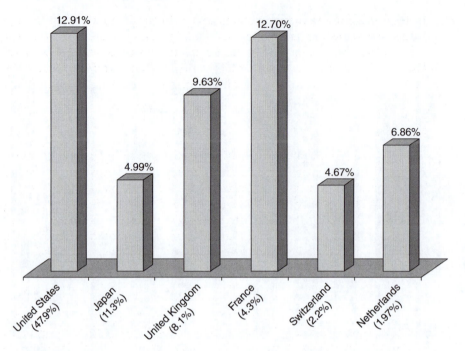

FIGURE 8.4 Allocation of German Funds to Equities in Other Countries; World Equity Market Share in Parentheses

Local Bias

People in the United States pick familiar foreign firms and bias their portfolios toward U.S. companies. Investors also tilt their portfolios toward local firms. For example, Coca-Cola's headquarters is located in Atlanta, Georgia. Investors living in Georgia own 16 percent of Coke,[17] and the majority of these investors live in Atlanta. Coke sells its products worldwide, but the people most familiar with the company own a large percentage of it.

This local bias is more general than just Coca-Cola stock holders. Professors Ivkovic and Weisbenner found that the average U.S. household invests 30 percent of its portfolio in companies headquartered within 250 miles of their home. Studies of international portfolio holdings show that both Swedish and Finnish investors also tilt their portfolios toward local firms.[18] In addition, people who move from one city to another within Sweden rebalance their portfolio. The farther away they relocate from a company, the more likely they are to sell that firm's stock. The new stocks they buy are biased toward being located in the area they have moved to. Interestingly, two languages are common in Finland: Finnish and Swedish. Firms may issue annual reports and other documents in either (or both) languages. Not only do investors in Finland tilt their portfolio toward local firms, they also tilt toward same-language firms. In short, investors seem to want to invest in companies that are familiar. Being more visible due to geographic proximity increases that familiarity.

Professional money managers also invest in the familiar. Even though U.S. professional investors have access to vast information sources and analysis tools, they tilt their portfolios toward local firms. This is especially true for local small firms and riskier firms. On average, the firms that a professional money manager buys are headquartered 100 miles closer to the manager's office than the typical U.S. company.[19]

Market Impacts

If a psychological bias impacts many people, then their aggregate behavior might impact the capital markets. For the familiarity bias, two interesting studies suggest that market returns are influenced by the local and home biases. Several scholars believe that the local bias of investors distort stock prices in regions of the United States.[20] In some places there are few companies available for investors. Since these firms are the "only game in town," they face little competition for local investors' dollars. The price pressure from investors concentrating on few firms may drive those firms' prices higher, relative to similar firms in other regions. They estimate that the price of a firm in the Deep South (relatively few firms) is 7.9 percent higher than a comparable firm in the middle Atlantic region (relatively many firms). This effect is smaller for the largest firms (4.1 percent), who have broader name recognition outside the area. The effect for the smallest 75 percent of the firms is much larger, 9.9 percent. In sort, the local bias of investors may skew the stock prices of smaller, less visible, regional firms.

In the international context, risk sharing between foreign and domestic investors lowers the risk in a particular stock market. Lower risks should result in lower expected returns due to the lower risk premium. Therefore, in the long run, national stock markets with lower home bias should have lower returns. In each of 38 countries, one study computes a measure of home bias and compares it to the country's MSCI index return.[21] Figure 8.5 shows a scatter plot of

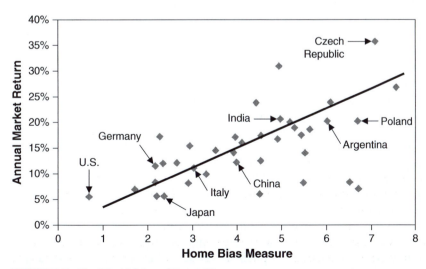

FIGURE 8.5 The World Price of Home Bias

home bias versus annual market return (during the period 1998–2007) for the 38 countries. Note the clear trend of higher home bias being associated with higher domestic market return. This creates a high cost of capital for the firm in countries with high degrees of home bias.

FAMILIARITY BREEDS INVESTMENT PROBLEMS

Which company are you most familiar with? People are generally most familiar with the company they work for. This familiarity causes employees to invest their pension money in the company stock. For example, a company 401(k) pension plan allows employees to invest money in options like a diversified stock fund, a bond fund, and money market instruments. One common option is the company's stock.

Traditional portfolio theory suggests that employees should diversify their retirement assets by selecting diversified stock, bond, and money market funds as needed according to their risk tolerance. Selecting the stock of one company is very poor diversification. In fact, since people already have their labor capital tied up in the company, to fully diversify, they should avoid investing their financial capital in that firm, too.

If your job and your retirement assets depend on one company, you could be in for a shock. Consider the plight of the employees of companies like Enron and Global Crossing. Measuring from the stock price peak values, the proportion of Enron employee 401(k) assets invested in Enron stock was 60 percent. The proportion of company stock in the Global Crossing 401(k) plan reached 53 percent. After Enron declared bankruptcy, thousands of its employees saw 401(k) losses total $1.3 billion. After the Enron and Global Crossing bankruptcies, the media wrote about employees who had their entire retirement fund invested in the company stock, which became worthless. Many of these people also lost their jobs.

Is it common for employees to invest their retirement money in their company's stock? Yes. In a survey of 246 of America's largest companies, 42 percent of the total 401(k) plan assets were invested in the company stock.[22] Employees themselves make this decision. They like investing in the company stock because it is familiar. This is dangerous!

When you are familiar with something, you have a distorted perception of it. Fans of a sports team think their team has a higher chance of winning than nonfans of the team. Likewise, investors look favorably on investments they are familiar with, believing they will deliver higher returns and have less risk than unfamiliar investments. For example, Americans believe the U.S. stock market will perform better than the German stock market; meanwhile, Germans believe their stock market will perform better.[23] Similarly, employees believe the stock of their employer is a safer investment than a diversified stock portfolio.[24]

Over concentrating a portfolio in only one stock is risky. However, employees do not want to believe that about the stock of their company. The Morningstar.com Web site asked investors this question: Which is more likely to lose half of its value, your firm or the overall stock market? It is far more likely that any single company would experience such a large price move than a diversified portfolio, especially the overall market. However, more than 1,000 investors responded to the question,[25] and only 16.4 percent of the respondents believed their company was riskier than the overall stock market. Of those investors without a college education, only 6.5 percent believed their company was riskier than the stock market. No one company is safer than a fully diversified portfolio like the overall stock market, so the familiarity bias clearly influences one's perception of risk.

The brain often uses the familiarity shortcut to evaluate investments. This can cause people to invest too much money in the stocks that are most familiar to them, like their employer's stock. Ultimately, this leads to a lack of diversification. In summary, investors allocate too much of their wealth to their employer, local companies, and domestic stocks.

COMBINING FAMILIARITY AND REPRESENTATIVENESS BIASES

Employees often compound the familiarity bias by combining it with the representativeness bias. Consider the ownership of company stock in employees' 401(k) plans. Employees tend to buy more of their company's stock after its price increases.[26] Employees who work for a company whose stock price increase ranked among the top 20 percent of all firms in the past five years allocated 31 percent of their contributions to the company stock. This compares to an allocation of only 13 percent to company stock in firms whose performance was in the worst 20 percent. The actual 401(k) asset allocation behavior of employees suggests that they use the past price trend (the representativeness bias) as a determinant for investing in the company stock (the familiarity bias). However, this is not a case of employees, as insiders, having good information about their firm. Firms with high employee pension plan ownership did not perform any better, on average, than those with low employee pension plan ownership.

Summary

Mental shortcuts, also called heuristic simplifications, help us analyze situations and make decisions quickly in our daily life. However, this process often leads us astray when analyzing decisions with risk and uncertainty. Since investing decisions involve substantial risk and uncertainty, our decisions are biased in predictable ways. The representativeness bias causes us to extrapolate the past and assume that good companies are good investments. The familiarity bias causes us to believe that firms we are familiar with are better investments than unfamiliar firms. Thus, we own more local firms and our employer's stock and few international stocks. Thus, these biases lead to low diversification and higher risks.

Questions

1. A statement found in every mutual fund prospectus is "Past performance is not indicative of future performance." Yet investors tend to use past performance as an important factor in making investment decisions. Why?

2. Why do investors in one country believe the return will be better and the risk is lower in their own country's stock market than in other countries' markets?

3. What are the home bias and foreign bias, and how are they related to familiarity?

4. How do the familiarity bias and the representativeness bias combine to influence the 401(k) pension plan choices of employees?

Notes

1. See discussions in the following sources: Hersh Shefrin, *Beyond Green and Fear: Understanding Behavioral Finance and the Psychology of Investing* (Boston: Harvard Business School Press, 2000); Hersh Shefrin and Meir Statman, "Making Sense of Beta, Size, and Book-to-Market," *Journal of Portfolio Management* (1995): 26–34; and Michael Solt and Meir Statman, "Good Companies, Bad Stocks," *Journal of Portfolio Management* (1989): 39–44.

2. See the empirical evidence in Werner De Bondt and Richard Thaler, "Does the Stock Market Overreact?" *Journal of Finance* 40(1985): 793–808, and the theoretical model of Nicholas Barberis, Andrei Shleifer, and Robert Vishny, "A Model of Investor Sentiment," *Journal of Financial Economics* 49(1998): 307–343.

3. See panels C and D of table 1 in Josef Lakonishok, Andrei Shleifer, and Robert Vishny, "Contrarian Investment, Extrapolation, and Risk," *Journal of Finance* 48(1994): 1541–1578.

4. Mary Bange, "Do the Portfolios of Small Investors Reflect Positive Feedback Trading?" *Journal of Financial and Quantitative Analysis* 35(2000): 239–255.

5. Werner De Bondt, "Betting on Trends: Intuitive Forecasts of Financial Risk and Return," *International Journal of Forecasting* 9(1993): 355–371.

6. Werner De Bondt and Richard Thaler, "Does the Stock Market Overreact?" *Journal of Finance* 40(1985): 793–808.

7. Warren Bailey, Alok Kumar, and David Ng, "Behavioral Biases of Mutual Fund Investors," *Journal of Financial Economics* 102(2011): 1–27.

8. Ivo Welch, "Views of Financial Economists on the Equity Premium and on Professional Controversies," *Journal of Business* 73(2000): 501–537; Ivo Welch, "The Equity Premium Consensus Forecast Revisited," Cowles Foundation discussion paper no. 1325, September 2001.

9. Chip Heath and Amos Tversky, "Preferences and Beliefs: Ambiguity and Competence in Choice Under Uncertainty," *Journal of Risk and Uncertainty* 4(1991): 5–28.

10. Much of this discussion is adapted from Gur Huberman, "Familiarity Breeds Investment," *Review of Financial Studies* 14(2001): 659–680.

11. John R. Nofsinger and Abhishek Varma, "Individuals and Their Local Utility Stocks: Preference for the Familar," *Financial Review* 47(2012): 423–443.

12. Joshua Coval and Tobias Moskowitz, "Home Bias at Home: Local Equity Preference in Domestic Portfolios," *Journal of Finance* 54(1999): 2045–2073.

13. Jun-Koo Kang and Rene Stulz, "Why Is There a Home Bias? An Analysis of Foreign Portfolio Equity Ownership in Japan," *Journal of Financial Economics* 46(1997): 3–28.

14. Kalok Chan, Vicentiu Covrig, and Lilia Ng, "What Determines the Domestic Bias and Foreign Bias? Evidence from Mutual Fund Equity Allocations Worldwide," *Journal of Finance* 60(2005): 1495–1534.

15. Kai Li, "Confidence in the Familiar: An International Perspective," *Journal of Financial and Quantitative Analysis* 39(2004): 47–68.

16. Norman Strong and Xinzhong Xu, "Understanding the Equity Home Bias: Evidence from Survey Data," *Review of Economics and Statistics* 85(2003): 307–312.

17. N. Deogun, "The Legacy: Roberto Goizueta Led Coca-Cola Stock Surge, and Its Home Prospers," *Wall Street Journal* (October 20, 1997).

18. See Zoran Ivković and Scott Weisbenner, "Local Does as Local Is: Information Content of the Geography of Individual Investors' Common Stock Investments," *Journal of Finance* 60(2005): 267–306; Massa Massa and Andrei Simonov, "Hedging, Familiarity and Portfolio Choice," *Review of Financial Studies* 19(2006): 633–685; Andriy Bodnaruk, "Proximity Always Matters: Local Bias When the Set of Local Companies Changes," *Review of Finance*, 13(2009): 629–656; and Mark Grinblatt and Matti Keloharju, "How Distance, Language, and Culture Influence Stockholdings and Trades," *Journal of Finance* 54(2001): 1053–1073.

19. Joshua Coval and Tobias Moskowitz, "Home Bias at Home: Local Equity Preference in Domestic Portfolios," *Journal of Finance* 54(1999): 2045–2073.

20. Harrison Hong, Jeffrey Kubik, and Jeremy Stein, "The Only Game in Town: Stock-Price Consequences of Local Bias," *Journal of Financial Economics* 90(2008): 20–37.

21. Sie Ting Lau, Lilian Ng, and Bohui Zhang, "The World Price of Home Bias," *Journal of Financial Economics* 97(2010): 191–217.

22. E. Schultz, "Color Tile Offers Sad Lessons for Investors in 401(k) Plans," *Wall Street Journal* (June 5, 1996); E. Schultz, "Workers Put Too Much in Their Employer's Stock," *Wall Street Journal* (September 13, 1996).

23. M. Kilka and M. Weber, "Home Bias in International Stock Return Expectations," *Journal of Psychology and Financial Markets* 1(2000): 176–193.

24. K. Driscoll, J. Malcolm, M. Sirull, and P. Slotter, "1995 Gallup Survey of Defined Contribution Plan Participants," *John Hancock Financial Services* (November 1995).

25. Shlomo Benartzi, "Excessive Extrapolation and the Allocation of 401(k) Accounts to Company Stock," *Journal of Finance* 56(2001): 1747–1764.

26. Ibid.

CHAPTER
9

Social Interaction
and Investing

People learn through interacting with other people. We watch the behavior of others to interpret their beliefs, but mostly we enjoy the social interaction of conversation; that is, we like to talk. We talk about subjects that excite us, topics that interest us, and even topics that worry us. Talking is an important way to obtain information and detect emotional reactions, which help form our opinions.

Our culture has experienced at least one tremendous shift in what we talk about over the past couple of decades. I refer to investment talk. The *social norms* of investment chat have changed dramatically. It was not so long ago that people avoided talking about investing. Asking someone about his or her mutual funds or talking about your stocks just wasn't done in a social setting.

Now, investment talk is heard everywhere. The financial channel, CNBC, was launched only in April 1989, yet when you go out to lunch, you'll often find it is being shown on the television. Other financially oriented cable channels, such as CNN FN (Cable News Network Financial News) and Bloomberg TV, followed CNBC's launch. Now dozens of regional and national radio shows dedicated to investing are being aired. This change in our social norms has had a dramatic impact on our investment behavior. As more people talk about investing, others become interested, too.

This shift in our society has had a dramatic impact on investment levels. Consider that in 1992, 31.6 percent of American households had a defined contribution (DC) plan. By 2001, 66.5 percent had a DC plan. Finally, in 2004,

73.5 percent of households had a DC plan.[1] American households are having to make more investment decisions than ever before. The more we talk about investing, the more we do it.

TALKING THE TALK

Conversation allows for the rapid exchange of information, opinions, and emotions. This is important for the stock market and investing. Stock brokers converse with clients and other brokers. Analysts communicate with executives and managers, and they form local groups and associations to interact with each other. Institutional investors form groups for sharing information. Individual investors talk to family members, neighbors, colleagues, and friends about investing.

For example, a survey of 156 high-income investors showed that more than half the time that an investor becomes interested in a stock, it is because another person mentioned it.[2] In addition, the survey found that since buying the stock, the new investor had spoken to an average of 20 other people about the company.

Imitate Thy Neighbor's Portfolio

Because information is obtained and decisions are formed through talking with others, social people are more likely to learn about investing than less social people. As a consequence, highly social people are more likely to invest in the stock market or to participate in their 401(k) plan. A group of researchers studied the relationship between socially active households and participation in the stock market.[3] A social household is characterized as one in which its members interact with neighbors or attend church. The researchers used responses from a survey of 7,500 households in the Health and Retirement Study of Households. They found that social households are more likely to invest in the stock market than nonsocial households and that social households that live in areas with high stock market participation are even more likely to invest in the stock market if they are socially active. Therefore, the social interaction influence is magnified when the person is in the right environment—one that has investors in it.

Other scholars have extended this idea to investor portfolio holdings. They argue that information about investing will diffuse through neighborhoods from word-of-mouth effects.[4] Even though investors tend to hold few stocks in their brokerage accounts (median is 4), they still find a strong neighborhood effect. When a household's neighbor increases purchases in an industry by 10 percentage points, the household also increases purchases in the same industry by 2 percent. The effect is much stronger for purchases in stock of local companies. When your neighbor increases his or her purchases by 10 percent, you tend to increase yours by a matching amount. This neighborhood effect has been found using both stock brokerage data and IRS tax return data. The information diffusion seems stronger in states that are considered to be more social, indicating that the residents are more comfortable seeking advice from others.

SOCIAL ENVIRONMENT

You can be judged by the friends you keep, according to one old saying. But does your social group affect your wealth? The answer appears to be yes. People in a peer group tend to develop the same tastes and interests as well as the desire to live a similar lifestyle. Peer groups develop social norms according to the preferred beliefs of the group. Beliefs about investing are also a part of these social norms. If investing is not valued by the peer group, the conversation will rarely (if ever) turn toward investment topics. Another peer group might discuss stocks frequently. The social environment impacts one's investment decisions.

One common example is participation in a 401(k) retirement plan (or other contribution plan). Because of the tax advantages, contributing to a retirement plan is a wise decision. If the employer also contributes in some matching way, that is even better. Yet many (even most) people do not participate. Education and wage levels are determinants of participation in the 401(k) plan; however, the social norms of employees also impact the participation decision.

To illustrate how dramatic the peer effect can be, consider the participation rate of 436 university librarians studied by Esther Duflo and Emmanuel Saez.[5] These librarians work in 11 different buildings throughout campus. Librarians are highly educated people. In addition, they are specifically trained in how to find information. Surely, librarians should make the wise choice and contribute to their retirement plans. The participation rates for the librarians in each of the 11 buildings are shown in Figure 9.1. Note the large difference in participation rates. In one building, 73 percent of the librarians participate, but in a different building, only 14 percent participate.

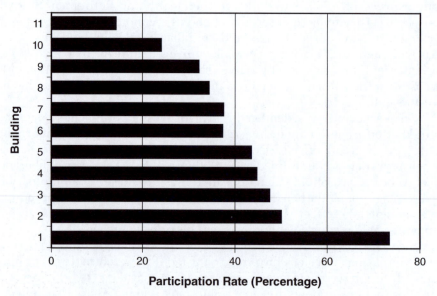

FIGURE 9.1 Pension Plan Participation Rates for 436 Librarians in 11 Locations

Differences in magnitude usually can be explained by groups having dissimilar education levels, salary levels, or both. People with higher education levels and higher wages are more likely to participate in a 401(k) pension plan. However, this study concerned only librarians, so they all have a relatively similar level of education and wages.

Because librarians are such a homogeneous group, the large variation in participation rates is striking. One explanation for the large differences is the social norms of each building. The social norms of each peer group develop over time. The norms in some buildings included in this study developed to value retirement plans, but in other buildings the norms developed such that participation in the retirement plan is not valued.

However, in this study, Duflo and Saez have no direct evidence of librarians influencing each other in the workplace. So they followed up this study with another retirement plan experiment at a large university in which a random sample of people from all the departments were invited to a benefits information fair.[6] At the fair, participants were encouraged to contribute to their defined contribution plan. Here is how the experiment worked. Of all the people who were invited, a small subset were told in advance that they were selected to receive a $20 reward for attending. Consider three groups: (1) winners of the reward, (2) nonwinners in a department with a reward winner, and (3) nonwinners in departments without any winners of the reward. It is not surprising that the winners had the highest attendance rate at the fair. Their attendance was five times greater than the third group (nonwinners in nonreward departments). What is surprising is that the people in group 2 (the nonwinners in a department with a winner) were three times more likely to attend the fair than people in group 3, even though neither of the groups received the reward. Why would the group 2 people want to go to the fair so much more than the group 3 people? Since they socially interact with the reward winners in their department, they learn of others planning to attend and may even interpret the giving away of a reward as a signal that the information at the fair is important. This effect continued past the fair and influenced decisions to contribute. The resulting contribution rate for people in group 2 was higher than those in group 3.

INVESTMENT CLUBS

One example of the socialization of investing is the rapid growth of investment clubs. An investment club is a group of family members, friends, or coworkers who have banded together to pool their money and invest it in the stock market. Frequently, the clubs are all men or all women. These groups typically meet once per month and discuss potential stock investments. Every month, the members each contribute some nominal amount ($20–$100), which is pooled and invested.

The creation of investment clubs is fostered through the National Association of Investors Corporation (NAIC). Although not all clubs are members of the NAIC, the organization boasted 35,810 clubs and 537,150 total members by the end of 2000. This is a substantial increase from the 7,087 clubs registered in 1990. However, after the financial crisis, the number of clubs dropped to 8,600 in 2009.

Investment Club Performance

How do most investment clubs perform? The financial press has made frequent claims suggesting that anywhere from 60 percent to two-thirds of the investment clubs beat the market. If true, this figure would be impressive given that most mutual funds don't routinely beat the market.

However, it is unlikely that these figures accurately reflect the performance of most investment clubs. The claims come from annual surveys of clubs by the NAIC. Consider the problems with this type of survey. First, the clubs have to properly calculate their annualized return.

Second, which clubs respond to the survey? If you were the treasurer of a club, when would you respond to a survey by the NAIC? You would be far more likely to fill out the survey if your club's returns were high and avoid filling out the survey if the returns were low. The psychological biases of seeking pride and avoiding regret suggest this behavior (see Chapter 3). Indeed, only 5–10 percent of the clubs return the NAIC survey. It is likely that these are the clubs that calculated a high return. Therefore, the survey results represent only the more successful clubs (at best) and are probably totally misrepresentative of all clubs (at worst).

To get a more objective view of investment club performance, the actual stock holdings of 166 investment clubs using a national discount broker were examined over a five-year period.[7] As Figure 9.2 shows, the results are not good. During this five-year period, the Standard & Poor's 500 Index earned an average 18 percent return annually. The clubs averaged a gross return of 17 percent per year. The return net of expenses was only 14.1 percent, so the clubs substantially underperformed the market.

Although media reports suggest that more than 60 percent of the clubs beat the market, it appears that 60 percent actually underperform the market. Indeed,

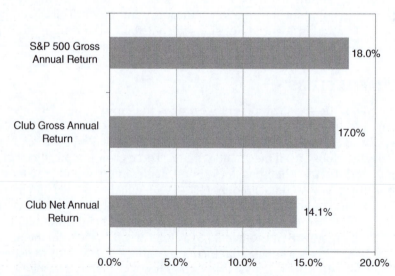

FIGURE 9.2   Investment Club Performance Versus Market Performance

the investing behavior of these clubs shows some of the same characteristics of psychological biases as individuals do. Specifically, trading behavior is consistent with overconfidence (Chapter 2) and the disposition effect (Chapter 3).

Investment Clubs and Social Dynamics

Although a club's purpose is to create an environment for learning about investing and achieving good returns, most clubs also serve a social purpose; that is, the meetings themselves provide a pretense for family members or friends to get together. Members tend to like the idea of sharing research skills and knowledge about the market while socializing on a regular basis.

The social dynamics of the club play an important role in its investment success. Although some clubs invest as a pretense to socialize, other clubs take their stock picking seriously. For example, the Klondike Investment Club of Buffalo, Wyoming, was rated the number one investment club in America one year by *Value Line*.[8] The 18 members of the club come from all walks of life. Some are young and some are old; some are blue-collar workers and some are white-collar workers; and some have advanced degrees; and others are business owners.

What is the secret of their success? The Klondikers exercise a high degree of investment formality. For example, this group requires all investment decisions to be made with the help of a rigorous report produced by the sponsoring member. They rely on research, not just stories about a firm. This is important because the approach helps the club avoid some psychological biases. Decisions are based on reason and logic rather than emotion.

Other investment clubs are formed with social interaction as their primary objective. Consider the California Investors Club, which was founded by a group of retired friends who had worked together for many years. Although their social events such as the Christmas party and a daylong golf outing are planned in great detail, their investment decisions are often made without much analysis.[9] Discussion frequently centers on hot tips and speculations; thus, the club frequently buys at the top and later sells at the bottom. As a consequence, the club has earned a poor return. The informality of this club allows each member's psychological biases to combine with those of the others and be magnified.

THE MEDIA

A large part of our social environment is the media, with various venues and media shows competing for our attention. If the news isn't well written or well told, the audience will pick up a different paper or change the channel. Business and investment writers keep us interested by telling a good story. Reporters also search for the best sound bite to quote. By its very nature, the sound bite is short and catches our attention, but it cannot convey any serious investment analysis; it is designed to convey a story. Most of the time, the media exacerbate our bias toward storytelling and away from formal investment analysis.

Although the media provide us with information and expert opinions, the experts express themselves through one-line explanations and quips. Many of these experts have access to research departments and tremendous analysis tools. Surely, we assume, their opinions are based on significant analysis. However, they rarely talk about the actual analysis, so we get the impression that investment analysis is simply storytelling. By trying to appeal to our interests and emotions, the media naturally gravitate toward the active investment decisions of stock selection and market timing.

Yet, media stories appear to impact investor behavior and stock prices even when it provides no new information. Paul Tetlock examined the market reaction to the daily "Abreast of the Market" column in the *Wall Street Journal*.[10] Tetlock categorizes each column by its level of pessimism for the stock market. High levels of pessimism or optimism in the morning article lead to unusually high trading later that day. The Dow Jones Industrial Average earned 0.25 percent more during the day after highly optimistic articles than highly pessimistic articles. However, these articles do not appear to have provided any lasting information. For example, the downward pressure on stock prices after a pessimistic column is reversed during the next few days of trading. While entertaining, the "Abreast of the Market" column does not seem to provide any new information to the market. Nevertheless, investors seem to trade as if it does.

Paul Tetlock also examined the pricing impact of stale news in general (not just the Abreast of the Market column).[11] He concludes that it is individual investors who react to news articles that contain old, previously released information. Stocks dominated by individual investors, not institutions, experience a significant return on the stale news day that is reversed over the following days. Not only do investors sometimes fail to distinguish between old information and new information in news, the financial media commonly transmit stale news.

Language

"The difference between the right word and the almost right word is the difference between lightning and the lightning bug."—Mark Twain.

Words are inherently less objective than numbers. Thus, they might influence investor judgment in different ways. Not all words have the same impact on the reader. Some words create vivid imagery that is emotionally interesting. Are investors' judgments different in learning that "Apple's sales jumped" versus "Apple's sales increased"? What about commentary like "very impressive" versus "exceeded the expectations"? Are we susceptible to hype?

An interesting experiment examined the impact of positive vivid words on people during a bull market and negative vivid words during a bear market.[12] During the context of a bull market, subjects were divided into those with long stock positions and those with short stock positions. Thus, those with short market positions are contrarian to the trend and general consensus. Within each long/short group, people were given positive news framed in either vivid or pallid phrases and then asked for a forecast. We should expect that people with long positions during a bull market will give higher predictions about the future than the contrarians with short positions. But which group is more influenced by the hype?

The study reports that the people with long positions during a bull market give similar predictions when given either vivid or pallid phrases. However, the contrarian people's predictions are impacted by the hype words. Those with short positions during the bull market give higher predictions when presented with vivid words compared to being shown pallid words. The experiment was redone and framed in a bear market. Here, the people with short positions are consistent with trend and consensus and the people with long positions are the contrarians. Vivid and pallid negative news treatments were administered. Again, it is the people with contrarian positions that were sensitive to the choice in words. Interestingly, vivid language, or hype, does not stoke the beliefs of those who already believe in the popular consensus. Instead, it is the contrarian investors who are sensitive to the vivid language.

SPEED IS NOT OF THE ESSENCE

If you watch the financial and business news cable channels, you are bombarded with commercials suggesting that in investing, the slow die first. You need the fastest Internet provider so that you can subscribe to the fastest news provider and trade on the fastest online brokerage system. For a while, CNBC even perpetuated this idea by timing and reporting the responsiveness of the major online brokerages.

Making split-second decisions after news reports is not investing; it is trading. Trading is like gambling in that it fosters strong emotional responses. This need for speed magnifies psychological biases.

Consider the simple mistakes that occur when people make split-second decisions. On April 11, 1997, the *Financial Times* ran a story that the Czech Value Fund had invested in fraudulent companies and was facing big losses.[13] When the news reached the United States, the stock with the ticker symbol CVF fell by 32 percent on high volume. The problem was that CVF is the ticker for Castle Convertible Fund, not the Czech Value Fund. By the end of the day, the Castle Fund had mostly recovered, but that didn't help the investors who sold at the bottom. The errors of others can cause you problems.

On June 24, 1998, it was reported that AT&T had agreed to purchase Tele-Communications Inc. for $45.8 billion. The stock with the ticker symbol TCI jumped nearly 5 percent on the news on volume that was more than 37 times normal for the firm.[14] However, TCI is the ticker symbol for Transcontinental Realty Investors Inc., not Tele-Communications. Interestingly, this had occurred to TCI five years earlier when Bell Atlantic Corp. announced its intention to buy Tele-Communications.

A similar case of mistaken identity occurred repeatedly over a one-year period with people trying to buy MCI Communications stock on a string of takeover rumors. The New York Stock Exchange stock with the ticker symbol MCI was continually confused with the ticker symbol for MCI Communications, which is MCIC. The MCI ticker symbol is for MassMutual Corporate Investors, a closed-end fund.

The media outlets race to be the first to report these events. Investors then rush to trade on this news with a herd mentality. In this case, the social interaction has influenced people in a way that increases their natural biases.

HERDING

As you learn what other people think about various stocks, a social consensus forms. As people act on this consensus, a herd forms. Investor herding is not unlike that of the antelope. Antelope stay together in herds to protect themselves from predators. One minute the herd of antelope is doing nothing, and the next minute the herd is in full gallop. An antelope always has its eyes and ears open so that it knows what the other antelope are doing—it doesn't want to be left behind.

Investors also keep an eye and ear open to what other investors are doing. Many people watch CNBC every day or closely follow chat room postings on a favorite Web site. Active investors check their portfolio daily. When things start moving, investors everywhere know about it.

The problem with moving with the herd is that it magnifies the psychological biases. It causes one to make decisions that are based on the "feel" of the herd instead of the rigor of formal analysis. In addition, the feeling of regret on picking a loser (Chapter 3) is lower when you know that many others picked the same stock. Misery loves company.

Herding into Stocks

When many investors are influenced by their psychological biases in a common way, a herd forms and the overall market can be affected. This is best illustrated by the irrational exuberance for Internet companies in the late 1990s. Many investors and analysts have been puzzled by the extremely high valuations of Internet firms. For example, when the historical average price/earnings (P/E) ratio of the market is around 15, what was the justification for Yahoo!'s P/E of 1,300 or eBay's P/E of 3,300 in late 1999? Many analysts concluded that new valuation measures were needed for this new revolution in the economy.

Or consider the valuation of eToys,[15] an online toy retailer that went public in 1999. Shortly after the initial public offering, the high price of the stock created a total value of the firm of $8 billion. Typical of Internet companies, eToys had negative earnings of $28.6 million from $30 million in sales. The natural comparison for eToys is Toys "R" Us, the "old economy" leading toy retailer. Even though Toys "R" Us had profits of $376 million, it had a market value of only $6 billion; that is, Toys "R" Us had a lower market valuation than eToys even though it earned 12 times more in profits than eToys had in sales.

This is even more astounding when you realize that the barrier to entry for firms getting on the Web is low. As you might recall, young entrepreneurs started many of the Internet firms on only a shoestring budget. Indeed, Toys "R" Us quickly developed its own online retail capability, and eToys' market capitalization fell from $8 billion to $29 million.

"A Rose.com by Any Other Name"

Consider the extent of herding in Internet companies. One example is firms that changed their name to FancyNewName.com. Investors went dot-com crazy and scooped up shares of any company related to the Internet. The easiest way to determine whether a firm is related to the Internet is by its name.

Consider the case of Computer Literacy Inc., an online retailer of technology books. This firm changed its name to fatbrain.com because customers kept misspelling (or forgetting) its former Internet address, computerliteracy.com. Note that this firm was already providing its service over the Internet. The change was in name only, not in business strategy. But when word leaked out about the name change, the online stock discussion groups sizzled, and the stock climbed 33 percent in one day!

From mid-1998 to mid-1999, a total of 147 publicly traded companies changed to a new name with a dot-com or dot-net ending or a name that included the word *Internet*.[16] During the three weeks after a name change announcement, these firms' stock beat the market by an average of 38 percent. All kinds of firms got in on the action. Some of these firms were already pure Internet companies. They beat the market by 57 percent during the three weeks after the name changes. Other firms that changed their names had only some Internet experience. These firms earned 35 percent over the market. Some firms that changed their names were changing from a non-Internet to an Internet focus and beat the market by 16 percent. In fact, even firms with little or no Internet experience changed their names and enjoyed the large stock price increases. These firms had a non-Internet core business, and no evidence was available to show that these firms had the expertise or experience to be successful. Yet Net-crazy traders bid up their stock prices to such a degree that they beat the market by 48 percent. These huge increases in stock price did not diminish over the following three months. Investors appeared to be eager to throw money at Internet companies. Interestingly, after the dot-com bust period in 2000, 67 companies removed the dot-com reference from their name. This name change was associated with an average 64 percent return during the next two months.[17] Investors do appear to be affected by cosmetic changes.

Investors have been frequently fooled by other name changes, too. Some mutual funds change their name to reflect the previous period's "hot" style (like value, growth, small stocks, and so on). This name change causes 28 percent more money to flow into the fund than otherwise expected.[18] This new money flow even occurs for funds that change their name but do not improve upon their investment style or performance.

SHORT-TERM FOCUS

In active trading, your thoughts are more like those of a trader than an investor. Instead of buying a stock because you think the company's products, market share, and management will dominate in the future, you buy a stock because you think the price will rise during the next week, day, or hour. The firm's products, market share, and management become ancillary or even irrelevant. Take Sharon, for example, who was interviewed by the PBS show *Frontline*.[19] She invested her family's entire life savings into two tiny technology stocks, placing most of it in one firm. "To tell you the truth, I don't even know the name of it. I know the call letters are AMLN. It's supposed to double by August," she said. For the record, AMLN is the ticker symbol for Amylin Pharmaceuticals.

Faith

"Things are different this time. The old valuation measures are no longer appropriate." These are the types of comments that are often uttered during a period of extreme herding because the high prices cannot be justified with traditional measures. When the scale says you have gained 30 pounds, the problem is obvious—your scale no longer works. While investing with the herd, people invest on the basis of faith, not due diligence.

Social Validation

People want to talk about investing. Conversation about investments becomes popular at social occasions, and the online discussion groups heat up. The expansion of radio talk shows featuring investment discussions and the call-in questions to CNBC demonstrate how investing invades other parts of life.

Herding and overvaluation do not occur because of new economics or new technologies—they occur because of the human psyche. New economics and new technology are only the rallying cry for the herd. When overconfidence (see Chapter 2) is combined with emotions, a problem results. The problem is magnified when everyone is caught up in making psychology-biased decisions.

Summary

People learn through interacting with each other. We talk about our beliefs about investing and seek the opinions of others. The opinions of our neighbors, friends, and colleagues impact our decisions. This allows more social people to gain confidence in their investing activities. Investment clubs are a formalized process of investing socialization. But clubs with a more strict investment procedure have more success than clubs focused on social activities. One outcome of social interaction is that investors tend to herd into the same stocks.

The media transmits much of the information we use to make investment decisions. Vivid language, or hype, influences the investors with contrarian positions. Unfortunately, investors tend to react too quickly to news stories. In fact, individual investors react to news that contains stale information or news that contains much important information—like company name changes. Investors even rush in so quickly that they buy the wrong stock by mistake. This short-term focus can be costly.

Questions

1. How does one's level of social interaction influence the likelihood of investing in the stock market and the type of stocks purchased?
2. Give examples of investment club environments in which psychological biases are exacerbated. Give examples of environments or tools that help control the biases.
3. Does the use of vivid language moderate or exacerbate a price bubble?
4. Explain how investors have been fooled by investment name changes.
5. How did the media influence investors in the late 1990s to herd into marginal firms?

Notes

1. These figures originate from the Survey of Consumer Finances as reported by Craig Copeland, "Individual Account Retirement Plans: An Analysis of the 2004 Survey of Consumer finances," *Employee Benefit Research Institute Issue Brief* 293(2006).

2. Robert Shiller and John Pound, "Survey Evidence on Diffusion of Interest and Information Among Investors," *Journal of Economic Behavior and Organization* 12(1989): 47–66.

3. Harrison Hong, Jeffrey D. Kubik, and Jeremy C. Stein, "Social Interaction and Stock-Market Participation," *Journal of Finance* 59(2004): 137–163.

4. See Zoran Ivkovic and Scott Weisbenner, "Information Diffusion Effects in Individual Investor's Common Stock Purchases: Covet Thy Neighbors' Investment Choices," *Review of Financial Studies* 20:4(2007): 1327–1357 and Jeffery R. Brown, Zoran Ivkovic, Paul A. Smith, and Scott Weisbenner, "Neighbors Matter: Causal Community Effects and Stock Market Participation," *Journal of Finance* 63:3(2008): 1509–1531.

5. Esther Duflo and Emmanuel Saez, "Participation and Investment Decisions in a Retirement Plan: The Influence of Colleagues' Choices," *Journal of Public Economics* 85(2002): 121–148.

6. Esther Duflo and Emmanuel Saez, "The Role of Information and Social Interactions in Retirement Plan Decisions: Evidence from a Randomized Experiment," *Quarterly Journal of Economics* (August 2003): 815–841.

7. Brad M. Barber and Terrance Odean, "Too Many Cooks Spoil the Profits: Investment Club Performance," *Financial Analysts Journal* (January/February 2000): 17–25.

8. Tony Cook, "Six Moneymaking Lessons You Can Learn from America's Top Investing Club," *Money Magazine* 25(December 1996): 88–93.

9. Brooke Harrington, *Capital and Community: Investment Clubs and Stock Market Populism* (Cambridge University Press, Cambridge, 2004).

10. Paul Tetlock, "Giving Content to Investor Sentiment: The Role of Media in the Stock Market," *Journal of Finance* 62(2007): 1139–1168.

11. Paul Tetlock, "All the News That's Fit to Reprint: Do Investors React to Stale Information?" *Review of Financial Studies* 24(2011): 1481–1512.

12. Jeffrey Hales, Xi (Jason) Kuang, and Shankar Venkatatraman, "Who Believes the Hype? An Experimental Examination of How Language Affects Investor Judgments," *Journal of Accounting Research* 49(2011): 223–255.

13. "Czech Markets Watchdog Chief Forced to Quit," *Financial Times*, April 11, 1997, p. 3.

14. Michael S. Rashes, "Massively Confused Investors Making Conspicuously Ignorant Choices (MCI-MCIC)," *Journal of Finance* 56(2001): 1911–1927.

15. Andrew Edgecliffe, "eToys Surges After Listing," *Financial Times*, May 21, 1999, p. 29.

16. Michael Cooper, Orlin Dimitrov, and Raghavendra Rau, "A Rose.com by Any Other Name," *Journal of Finance* 56(2001): 2371–2388.

17. Michael Cooper, Ajay Khorana, Igor Osobov, Ajay Patel, and Raghavendra Rau, "Managerial Actions in Response to a Market Downturn: Valuation Effects of Name Changes in the Dot.Com Decline," *Journal of Corporate Finance* 11(2005): 319–335.

18. Michael Cooper, Huseyin Gulen, and Raghavendra Rau, "Changing Names with Style: Mutual Fund Name Changes and Their Effects on Fund Flow," *Journal of Finance* 60(2005): 2825–2858.

19. *Frontline*, January 4, 1997.

CHAPTER

10

Emotion and Investment Decisions

Traditional finance theory assumes that people make rational decisions to maximize their wealth in the face of risk and uncertainty. Because money is involved, reason and logic will overcome emotion and psychological biases, it would seem. Is this a good assumption? In reality, the situation might be just the opposite. Emotion might overcome reason when one is making a risky decision involving money.

FEELINGS AND DECISIONS

Psychologists and economists have examined the role of emotions in decision making. They call these feelings *affect*. They have found that unrelated feelings and emotions can affect decisions.[1] The term *unrelated* in this case means emotions that are not attributed to the decision. For example, you might be in a good mood because the sun is shining or because your favorite team just won. This good feeling can subsequently influence an investment decision. In addition, people who have stronger emotional reactions seem to let them impact their financial decisions. Emotions interact with the cognitive evaluation process to eventually lead to a decision. At times, emotional reactions diverge from reason and logic to dominate the decision-making process. Indeed, the more complex and uncertain a situation is, the more emotions influence a decision.[2]

The central question then is: What is the relative importance of emotion and reason in decision making? It appears that emotions play a large role. For example, neurologist Antonio Damasio reported on patients who suffered damage to the ventromedial frontal cortices of the brain. This damage leaves intelligence, memory, and capacity for logic intact but impairs the ability to feel. Through various experiments, it was surmised that the lack of emotion in the decision-making process destroyed the ability to make rational decisions.[3] Indeed, these people became socially dysfunctional. Damasio concluded that emotion is an integral component of making reasonable decisions.

Consider how psychologists study the effect of moods on decisions. They have their subjects write an essay about a sad or happy event in their lives. Reliving the event through their writing puts the subjects in bad or good moods, respectively. This mood appears to affect their predictions about the future. People who are in a bad mood are more pessimistic about the future than people who are in a good mood; that is, the subjects who are in a good mood assign a higher probability of good things happening and a lower probability of bad things happening.

In one study, the people who were in a good mood believed they had an 84 percent chance that "Within the next year, I will meet a new person who will come to be a very good friend."[4] The people who were in a bad mood believed that the chance of this happening was only 51 percent. Alternatively, when asked for the probability that "I will be involved in a major automobile accident within the next five years," people who were in a bad mood thought the chance was 52 percent, and those who were in a good mood thought the chance was only 23 percent. People who are in a good mood view the future differently than people who are in a bad mood.

In addition to the importance of emotion, people are often insensitive to changes in the facts used in cognition. One such fact is the probability of outcomes. For example, people tend to treat the probability of winning a lottery of 1 in 10 million or 1 in 10,000 similarly when making a decision. Yet, one has a 1,000 times higher chance of happening. In particular, the decision to take a gamble is relatively insensitive to large changes in probability when the gamble evokes strong emotions. In short, emotions drive the process of complex decision making.

FEELINGS AND FINANCE

Financial decisions are complex and include risk and uncertainty. Thus, emotions can play a role in investment decision making. Consider the month-long experiment conducted at the MIT Laboratory for Financial Engineering.[5] Investors made trades and commented on their emotional state. The experimenters concluded that the investors who had the most intense emotional response to monetary gains and losses exhibited significantly worse trading performance. The emotional investor is a poor investor!

Background feelings, or mood, may also influence financial decisions. This is called the *misattribution bias*. That is, people often misattribute the mood (or affect) they are in to the financial decision at hand. If someone is in a good mood, he or she is more likely to be optimistic in evaluating an investment. Good (bad) moods will increase (decrease) the likelihood of investing in risky assets, like stocks. The misattribution bias has been examined in financial decisions in several ways.

Feelings Affect Investment Decisions

Consider that an investor's decision to buy or sell a stock is based on expectations. The traditional finance view is embodied by the rational expectations model, which assumes that investor expectations are derived from using tools such as fundamental analysis and modern portfolio theory. These tools require making certain assumptions about the future. What growth rate will the firm achieve over the next three years? What is its expected return, expected variance, and expected correlation with other assets? Even the most sophisticated investors do not agree about which methods produce the most accurate assumptions. The rational expectations model requires that investors resolve these uncertainties in an unbiased and rational way. Yet, evidence indicates that people make biased and nonrational choices driven by emotion and cognitive errors.

This is illustrated by an experiment conducted by Kuhnen and Knutson.[6] They have subjects play a game in which they must continuously choose between investing in a risky asset with known probabilities for each outcome and a risk-free. They play for money. Before playing, positive, neutral, or negative emotions are induced through seeing a possibly provocative image and discussing it. They find that being induced with positive emotions leads to riskier choices and more confidence in those choices. One reason for this confidence is that they do not fully incorporate information that contradicts their prior choices. Negative emotions lead to more risk-averse choices.

Even those investors who use quantitative methods such as fundamental analysis can be influenced by their mood. There is more than just unbiased numbers. Analysis includes educated guesswork about some assumptions. Some fundamental analysis techniques are more sophisticated than others, but they all involve assumptions about the future. To illustrate, consider the constant discount rate model taught to finance students around the world, $PV = D_1/(k - g)$. Investors must estimate the constant growth rate, g. Given the influence of mood on risky and uncertain decisions, the expected value of the growth rate may become biased. In turn, this biases the value computed in the model.

For this example, assume that the annual return, k, is known to be 11 percent, and there will be a long-term dividend growth rate of 5 percent. An investor who is in a good mood might optimistically overestimate the growth rate to be 7 percent. This would cause the investor to believe the stock is worth 50 percent more than the belief of an unbiased investor. The optimistic investor might purchase the stock thinking it is undervalued when in reality it is not.

Sunshine

For the past several decades, psychologists have been documenting how the sun affects our decisions. A lack of sunlight has been linked to depression and even suicide. Without the sun, we feel bad. When the sun is shinning, we feel good. This good mood makes us optimistic about our future prospects and affects our decision-making process.

Even our financial decisions may be affected by sunshine. For example, you will probably leave a bigger tip for your server at lunch if it is sunny outside. You do not even need to be outside to feel good about sunshine. One psychologist conducted an experiment at a large hotel where many of the rooms did not have windows.[7] When a guest from one of these interior rooms ordered room service, the server would mention the weather outside. The server received an average tip of 18.8 percent on rainy days. This increased to 24.4 percent on cloudy days, 26.4 percent on partially sunny days, and 29.4 percent on sunny days. People give a tip that is more than 50 percent higher on sunny days than on rainy days.

Can the happy mood of a sunny day affect investors and the stock market? If the sunshine puts investors in a good mood, they will be more optimistic about future prospects. Therefore, investors are more likely to buy stock than to sell stock on sunny days. If the tendency to buy rather than sell affects enough investors, the stock market itself could be affected. Two financial economists examined this possibility by looking at stock market returns and the weather in the financial cities of the world.[8] Specifically, they compared the daily return in 26 stock exchanges around the world to the weather in the 26 cities in which the stock markets were located.

These researchers used a weather scale with nine levels ranging from completely sunny to completely miserable. They found that the daily returns for sunny days are higher than the daily returns for nonsunny days. Indeed, the returns for the sunniest days are much higher than the returns for the most miserable days of weather. When they annualized the difference between the sunniest and worst days in all 26 cities, they found that sunny days outperformed miserable weather days by 24.6 percent per year.

The annualized difference in returns between sunny and miserable days is shown for several cities in Figure 10.1. The average for all 26 cities is also shown. Note that sunny days outperform on the New York Stock Exchange to the tune of 15 percent per year. Sunny days earn an annualized return of 22.1 percent

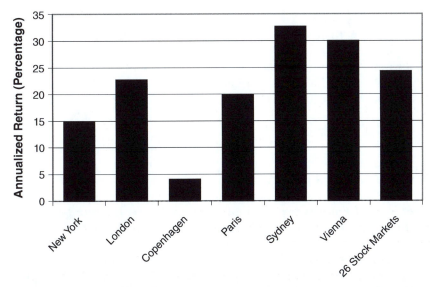

FIGURE 10.1 Annualized Difference in Return Between Sunny Days and Miserable Weather Days for Stock Markets Around the World

over miserable days in London, 4.1 percent in Copenhagen, and 19.7 percent in Paris. Not every day is sunny or miserable; most days are in between. However, this illustrates that the sun affects investors and the market.

Another way to examine the effect of sunshine on investor mood and behavior is to examine stock market returns by seasons. Psychologists have found that the decreasing amount of daylight during the fall and winter leads to depression in many people. This depression is called seasonal affective disorder (SAD). It is believed that 10 million Americans are afflicted with SAD and another 15 million suffer from a mild case of "winter blues." Remember that people who are in a bad mood or in a depressed state are more critical and pessimistic, and people who are in a good mood are more optimistic. This leads to greater risk taking by people who are in good moods than by people who are in bad moods.

If the decreasing length of daylight affects many investors, they will take less risk. Three financial economists investigated this possibility by studying seven stock markets around the world: Australia, Great Britain, Canada, Germany, New Zealand, Sweden, and the United States.[9] They found that stock returns are lower during the fall when daylight decreases until December 21, the longest night of the year. This effect is the strongest for stock markets that are farthest away from the equator (Sweden and Great Britain). Also consistent with this idea is that the effect occurs during the spring for markets in the southern hemisphere (Australia and New Zealand). Again, it appears that daylight (or the lack of it) affects our mood. This mood also affects our investment decisions, our decision-making process, and the amount of risk we are willing to take.

Negative Emotions

Just as investors can misattribute the positive feelings from sunlight, they can also misattribute the negative feelings from other factors in their environment. This section explores two examples: international sport competitions and the lunar cycle.

Historically, there has been a popular perception that lunar phases affect people's mood and behavior. The moon has long been associated with mental disorder. Indeed, the word *lunacy* links potential mental illness with the lunar cycle. Psychologists have reported correlations between the full moon and depressed mood. If the lunar cycle impacts investors, then they may value stocks less during a full moon relative to a new moon, thus causing a lower return around the full-moon period.

The returns in 48 stock markets around the world were investigated during the lunar cycle.[10] Stock returns were 3–5 percent lower per year during the seven days around the full moon than around a new moon. This effect is larger in emerging stock market countries than in developed countries. It is also stronger in stocks mostly held by individual investors. Investors do appear to misattribute the negative feelings associated with the full moon to their stock market decisions.

While the lunar cycle is predictable, the outcome of international sporting games is not. The outcome of soccer matches in the European or World Cups produce substantial mood swings in a large proportion of a country's population. Psychologists have found an increase in heart attacks, crimes, and suicides accompanying sporting losses. There is no evidence of positive behavior after wins. This is possibly because the reference point of many fans is that their team will win. Thus, a victory is a minimal deviation from the reference point, while a loss is a large deviation.

Two studies examined the stock market reactions to losses in popular sporting events.[11] The first paper examined stock returns in 39 countries to more than 1,100 soccer match outcomes. The day after a soccer game loss, the losing team's stock market declines an average –0.21 percent. If the game was a tournament elimination match, the decline is –0.38 percent (–0.49 percent in the World Cup). The stock market reaction is stronger in countries that have historically performed well in soccer. Declines of –0.19 and –0.21 percent are found after cricket and basketball losses. No stock market impact was found after victories. The second paper examines the returns of locally HQ teams after American football games. The companies located in the losing city underperform those in the winning city over the day after the game by 0.0575 percent. This effect is double when the games are critical or the losing team was favored to win. Now you know, it really is more than just a game! These results suggest that the stock market reacts to sudden changes in investor mood.

Optimism

Optimism skews a person's beliefs and judgments. Optimistic people believe they are less likely than average to experience disease and divorce or to be a victim of crime. This belief can cause the optimist to take unnecessary risks.

Consider the average cigarette smoker. The fact that smoking is hazardous to your health comes as no surprise to smokers. Warnings are printed on every pack and on TV commercials. Everyone knows that smoking increases the risk of lung cancer, but smokers optimistically believe they personally are at low risk for the disease. After all, you would not be very intelligent if you thought you were at high risk and smoked anyway. To help preserve one's self-image of being intelligent, smokers are optimistic about their chance of not getting lung cancer, which allows them to continue the hazardous behavior.

Investors who are in a good mood can also suffer from optimistic decisions. That is, investors can also believe that nothing bad is likely to happen to their stock picks. Optimism affects investors in two ways. First, optimistic investors tend to do less critical analysis in making their stock decisions. Second, optimists tend to ignore (or downplay) negative information about their stocks. In other words, the optimistic investor holds fast to the belief that a firm is great, even when negative news about the firm is revealed—just as the smoker downplays the risk of getting cancer after reading the warning label.

The price of a stock is frequently set by the optimistic investors. If many investors are optimistic about a stock and many are pessimistic, the price of the stock will be driven by the optimists. This is because the pessimists stay on the sideline, while the optimists buy. The optimists drive up the stock price with their buying. This makes the pessimists even more pessimistic, but staying on the sideline does not affect the price. A stock will have a large number of optimists and pessimists (as opposed to mostly unbiased investors) when there is a large degree of uncertainty about the prospects of the stock. The prospects of large, well-established firms have less uncertainty, so their stocks prices are generally more reflective of actual prospects than of optimistic prospects. For example, the business potential of General Electric, Procter & Gamble, and Intel are pretty well known and leave little room for a high degree of optimism and pessimism. For firms with a high degree of uncertainty, optimists tend to set the stock price until that uncertainty is resolved. This resolution usually includes a downward revision of optimism and a decline in the stock price.

Rampant optimism, or irrational exuberance, can be found in the stock market. Consider the case of Palm and 3Com. 3Com was a profitable firm that sold computer network systems and services. One of the products it developed in its Palm subsidiary was the handheld computer known as the Palm Pilot. 3Com decided to spin off Palm into its own company. The plan was to issue 4 percent of the shares of Palm in an initial public offering (IPO), sell 1 percent of the shares to a consortium of firms, and distribute the remaining 95 percent of the Palm shares to 3Com stockholders. On March 2, 2000, 3Com sold the 5 percent of Palm in the IPO. The other 95 percent of the Palm stock was to be distributed later in the year as 1.5 shares of Palm for every 1 share of 3Com stock owned. So if you owned 1 share of 3Com stock, after the distribution you would own 1.5 shares of Palm and still own 1 share of 3Com.

By the end of the IPO day, the newly issued shares of Palm traded at $95.06. Because 1 share of 3Com would receive 1.5 shares of Palm, the 3Com stock should have been worth a minimum of $142.59 (this is equal to $1.5 \times \$95.06$) from the value of the Palm shares alone. 3Com's non-Palm operations also had value. These businesses were earning $750 million in annual profits for 3Com,[12] so the 3Com stock price should have been much higher than $142.59. However, 3Com stock closed at only $81.81 per share that day.

If you wanted to own Palm stock, you could have bought 3Com stock and gotten the Palm stock for an effective price of $54.54 (which is equal to $81.81 \div 1.5$) per share and owned the 3Com stock for free. Either 3Com stock was priced too low or Palm stock was priced too high. Because 3Com was a larger, better-established firm and Palm was a new firm in an uncertain environment, it is likely that optimistic investors affected the Palm stock. All relevant information about Palm and 3Com was readily available before the IPO. The day after the IPO, the *Wall Street Journal* and the *New York Times* ran articles highlighting the strange mispricing. Yet, the mispricing continued for months. The value of the embedded Palm stock in the 3Com stock continued to be worth more than the 3Com stock itself for two more months (until May 9). Again, optimistic investors ignored, or minimized, bad news about their firms.

Although the 3Com/Palm example is interesting, it is not unique. For example, HNC Software spun off Retek on November 17, 1999; Daisytek spun off PFSWeb on December 1, 1999; and Methode Electronics spun off Stratos Lightwave on June 26, 2000. In all three cases, optimistic investors drove the new company's stock price up. Just like 3Com and Palm, the price of the parent company's stock was less than the embedded value of the spin-off firm's stock price. These three other cases shared another thing with 3Com and Palm.

In each case, the new company's stock price fell by 50 percent or more during the ensuing six months.

Other similar examples can be cited. Some companies do not entirely spin off a new company; that is, sometimes the parent company will keep some stock of the subsidiary instead of distributing it to the shareholders. The optimism about the subsidiary can get so great that the price gets run up and mispricing results between the parent and the subsidiary. For example, in September 1999, Flowers Industries owned 55 percent of the shares of Keebler Foods. The stock price of Keebler was such that its total market capitalization (number of shares of stock times the stock price) was $2.50 billion. Because Flowers owned 55 percent of Keebler, its ownership was worth $1.38 billion, yet the total market capitalization of Flowers was only $1.36 billion. Flowers's stock price was such that its market capitalization was lower than the holdings of just one of its assets, Keebler. The value of the other assets was approximately $1 billion. Clearly, either Keebler was severely overpriced or Flowers was underpriced. This phenomenon has occurred to several firms and illustrates the price inflation of stocks driven by optimism.[13] Buying a stock whose price is driven up by optimism usually leads to losses as the optimism unwinds—and eventually, the optimism always unwinds.

This investor mania caused a price bubble in the 1990s. In 2000, the bubble burst. The technology-laden NASDAQ (National Association of Securities and Dealers Automated Quotation) composite stock index experienced a 54 percent decline from its peak in March to its low in December 2000. Internet-focused stock indexes such as the TSC Internet Sector Index declined by 79 percent over the same period. In comparison, the Dow Jones Industrial Average increased by 4 percent.

SENTIMENT

The previous examples of emotions impacting the market can be characterized as either the social misattribution of good and bad feelings to stock market optimism and pessimism or the specific excitement of speculating on an individual company. However, many people have observed that the general level of optimism and pessimism, or social mood, changes over time.[14] Indeed, it appears that investors tend to be most optimistic at the market top and most pessimistic at the market bottom (see the representativeness bias in Chapter 7). The investment industry refers to this fluctuating social mood as market *sentiment*. If individual investors get too optimistic (pessimistic) during market tops (bottoms), then knowing the general sentiment might allow for the prediction of returns.

An example of seasonal optimism in society occurs during the month long period of Ramadan in Muslim countries. Ramadan is a time for fasting, reflection, self-reformation, giving, worship, social awareness, and a closer relationship with fellow Muslims around the world. This enhances their satisfaction with life and encourages optimistic beliefs. Three scholars investigated whether this positive sentiment impacts the stocks returns in 14 Muslim countries.[15] They show that over a 19 year period, Ramadan is associated with an average return of 3.17 percent (my computation from their results). This compares to an average total return during the other 11 months of the year of 3.96 percent. This suggests that nearly half of the annual return occurs in just the one month of Ramadan!

There are many measures of investor sentiment. Consider the discount to closed-end mutual funds. A closed-end fund is similar to its more popular cousin, the open-end fund, except that its shares trade on the stock exchanges. Since the stocks held in the closed-end fund portfolio are known, the value of each fund share is also known and is called the net asset value (NAV). Interestingly, closed-end funds generally trade for prices below their NAV. The size of the difference, or discount, is a measure of sentiment. When individual investors are optimistic, the demand for these funds increases and the discount declines. Pessimistic investors sell the funds, and the discount increases. Other popular measures are the number of IPOs being conducted and the magnitude of their first-day return. These values are higher when sentiment is high.[16]

The argument for why investor sentiment should not impact market prices is that wealthy and smart investors look to trade against moody investors to capture the mispricings they create as profits. This process is known as *arbitrage*. However, arbitrage is difficult to do in stocks that are hard to value. Malcolm Baker and Jeffrey Wurgler propose that the impact of investor sentiment will be most noticeable in these speculative stocks.[17] Companies that might meet this definition are ones that are small, young, volatile, unprofitable, distressed, or have extreme growth potential. They examine the influence of investor sentiment on these stocks by measuring the sentiment at the beginning of the year and reporting monthly stock returns during the following year. They hypothesize that the returns of these speculative stocks will be low (high) after high (low) measures of sentiment.

Figure 10.2 shows the average monthly return during the year after positive (or high) sentiment and after negative (or low) sentiment. Baker and Wurgler combined six different sentiment measures to create one sentiment index from 1963 to 2001. Notice from the figure that the speculative stocks (small companies, young companies, or risky companies) all have much higher monthly returns after beginning the year with negative sentiment than with positive sentiment. For example, small stocks earn 2.37 percent per month after a low sentiment measure and only 0.73 percent per month after a high measure. This large difference is not seen in large stocks. The youngest firms earn 1.77 percent per month after beginning the year with low sentiment and only 0.25 percent when starting with high sentiment. The returns for the most volatile firms are 2.41 and 0.30 percent per month, respectively. The returns of older firms and low-risk firms do not exhibit this pattern.

These results suggest that optimistic investors bid up speculative stocks to overvalued levels. When the optimism becomes high, so does the stock price. From these high levels, the stocks subsequently earn a lower return. Pessimistic investors avoid speculative stocks, which fall to a low level. Subsequent to high pessimism levels, these stocks earn a high return. Therefore, speculative stock prices are more sensitive to sentiment than firms with long histories, stable dividends, and tangible assets.

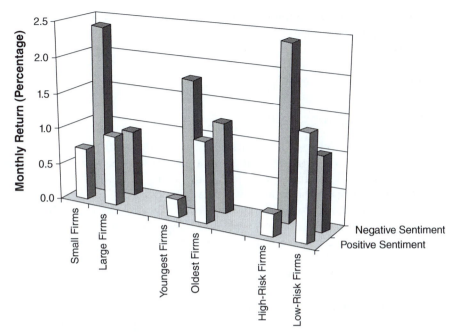

FIGURE 10.2 Monthly Returns After Positive and Negative Sentiment Levels for Speculative and Nonspeculative Firms

MARKET BUBBLES

The more things change, the more *people* stay the same. Market bubbles are not a recent phenomenon, nor are they uncommon.

One of the most impressive market bubbles occurred in Holland in the 1630s.[18] What makes that bubble so amusing is that the highly sought-after commodity was the tulip bulb. Over a five-year period, tulip bulb mania inflated bulb prices to the point where one bulb was worth 10 times a yoke of oxen. A tulip bulb costing nearly $100,000? Then an out-of-town sailor inadvertently popped the tulip bulb price bubble. Mistaking the bulb for an onion, he ate it. Wondering whether the bulbs were worth the high prices, panic erupted; within a week, the bulbs were almost worthless.

Modern market bubbles have common elements. Given the statement that follows, how would you fill in the blank?

We are in a new era. _____ has ushered in a new type of economy. Those stuck in the old ways will quickly fall away. Traditional company valuation techniques do not capture the value of this revolution.

You probably answered "the Internet." However, if you lived in 1850, you would have said "the railroad." If you lived in the 1920s, you might have said "the Federal Reserve System" or "the radio." In the mid-1950s, the answer would have been "the New Deal." Even as recently as 1990, you might have said "biotechnology." In each case, this rationalization accompanied a great bull market and preceded a great decline. The point is that price bubbles are not uncommon, nor is each one unique.

THE THRILLS OF INVESTING

Some people may invest or trade because they like to do so. It provides excitement or is entertaining. Indeed, some people may even get a thrill from trading. For these individuals, trading is similar to gambling. The desire to gamble has deep roots in the human psyche and its evidence can be traced back centuries. The investing world has ripe opportunities for gambling. Securities like stocks have risk, uncertainty, and the chance for making large sums of money. Thus, people could behave like gamblers and seek sensation through their brokerage accounts.

What kind of investment activities might we expect to see from a sensation seeker? Gamblers like to make active decisions. Being an active participant is important to the seeking of sensation. In a brokerage account, that would lead to lots of trading. In addition, those looking for entertainment from trading would seek out stocks with lottery-like characteristics. These characteristics include a low price and a high return volatility. That is, gambles like the lottery have a very low cost and a very low probability of winning a large amount of money. Investors seeking entertainment might try to find stocks with those characteristics. Three interesting studies explore sensation-seeking investors and their behavior.

Decades of research shows that the most common lottery player is a young, poor, less-educated, single man who is from a minority group, lives in an urban area and has a nonprofessional job. Alok Kumar studied U.S. investors' broker-age accounts and found that these same socioeconomic characteristics describe those who seek lottery-type stocks.[19] In addition, people in states with a lottery and who live in areas with a higher concentration of Catholics also have a higher propensity for lottery-type stocks. Investors in Germany were surveyed as to how much they enjoyed investing and gambling. Those who enjoyed them more traded twice as much as nongamblers.[20]

Professors Mark Grinblatt and Matti Keloharju studied investors in Finland. Their unique dataset allowed them to merge stock brokerage data with other databases.[21] For example, they knew how many speeding tickets the investors had received and if the investor was male, they had access to psychology tests given during mandatory military service. Investors who are sensation seeking in one area, like playing poker, tend to also be sensation seek-ing in other areas. Thus, they compared the activities of those investors who are prone to sensation seeking (a higher number of speeding tickets) with those who are not. After controlling for other investors characteristics, they found that sensation seekers trade more than other investors. They seem to derive some entertainment from trading.

Most of this chapter has been about how emotions impact peoples' decisions in investing and other economic events. Interestingly, it turns out that some people invest to elicit certain emotions. They trade specific types of stocks to feel the sensations associated with gambling. In order to protect a sensation-seekers' wealth, that person might set up a "play" brokerage account with a small portion of the portfolio. That way, they can satisfy their need for entertainment and yet protect the larger portion of their portfolio from bad, gambling-like decisions.

Summary

Emotions are an important part of the decision-making process. This is especially true for decisions that involve a high degree of uncertainty, such as investment decisions. Sometimes, emotion can overcome logic in this process. Too much optimism leads investors to underestimate risk and overestimate expected performance.

Optimistic investors tend to seek good-story stocks and be less critical. Pessimistic investors tend to be more analytical. Extended, extreme optimism can cause price bubbles. On the other hand, some sensation-seeking investors look for the gambling-like emotions from excessive trading.

Questions

1. How might being in a good mood or bad mood influence an investor's decisions?
2. How can optimism and pessimism affect the results of quantitative asset pricing?
3. Explain the misattribution bias and its effect on investment behavior.
4. Design an investment strategy to profit from the impact of investor sentiment on the market.
5. What kind of investing activities would you expect from a person prone to sensation seeking?

Notes

1. For example, see George Loewenstein, Elki U. Weber, Christopher K. Hsee, and Ned Welch, "Risk as Feelings," *Psychological Bulletin* 127(2001): 267–286 and Paul Slovic, Melissa Finucane, Ellen Peters, and Donald MacGregor, "The Affect Heuristic," in *Heuristics and Biases: The Psychology of Intuitive Judgment*, ed. T. Gilovich, D. Griffin, and D. Kahneman (New York: Cambridge University Press, 2002), 397–420.

2. Joseph P. Forgas, "Mood and Judgment: The Affect Infusion Model (AIM)," *Psychological Bulletin* 117(1995): 39–66.

3. Antonio Damasio, *Descartes' Error: Emotion, Reason, and the Human Brain* (New York: Avon, 1994); Antonio Damasio, D. Tranel, and H. Damasio, "Individuals with Sociopathic Behavior Caused by Frontal Damage Fail to Respond Autonomically to Social Stimuli," *Behavioral Brain Research* 41(1990): 81–94.

4. William Wright and Gordon Bower, "Mood Effects on Subjective Probability Assessment," *Organizational Behavior and Human Decision Processes* 52(1992): 276–291.

5. Andrew Lo, Dmitry Repin, and Brett Steenbarger, "Fear and Greed in Financial Markets: A Clinical Study of Day-Traders," *American Economic Review* 95(2005): 352–359.

6. Camelia M. Kuhnen and Brian Knutson, "The Influence of Affect on Beliefs, Preferences, and Financial Decisions," *Journal of Financial and Quantitative Analysis* 46(2011): 605–626.

7. Bruce Rind, "Effect of Beliefs About Weather Conditions on Tipping," *Journal of Applied Social Psychology* 26(1996): 137–147.

8. See David Hirshleifer and Tyler Shumway, "Good Day Sunshine: Stock Returns and the Weather," *Journal of Finance* 58(2003): 1009–1032 and Melanie Cao and Jason Wei, "Stock Market Returns: A Note on Temperature Anomaly," *Journal of Banking and Finance* 29(2005): 1559–1573.

9. Mark Kamstra, Lisa Kramer, and Maurice Levi, "Winter Blues: A Sad Stock Market Cycle," *American Economic Review* 93(2003): 324–343.

10. Kathy Yuan, Lu Zheng, and Qiaoqiao Zhu, "Are Investors Moonstruck? Lunar Phases and Stock Returns," *Journal of Empirical Finance* 13(2006): 1–23.

11. See Alex Edmans, Diego Garcia, and Oyvind Norli, "Sports Sentiment and Stock Returns," *Journal of Finance* 62(2007): 1967–1998 and Shao-Chi Chang, Sheng-Syan Chen, Robin K. Chou, and Yueh-Hsiang Lin, "Local Sports Sentiment and Returns of Locally Headquartered Stocks: A Firm-level Analysis," *Journal of Empirical Finance* 19(2012): 309–318.

12. For additional discussion, see Brad Barber and Terrance Odean, "The Internet and the Investor," *Journal of Economic Perspectives* 15(2001): 41–54. See also Gur Huberman and Tomer Regev, "Contagious Speculation and a Cure for Cancer: A Nonevent That Made Stock Prices Soar," *Journal of Finance* 56(2001): 387–396.

13. Bradford Cornell and Qiao Liu, "The Parent Company Puzzle: When Is the Whole Worth Less Than One of the Parts?" *Journal of Corporate Finance* 7(2001): 341–366.

14. John Nofsinger, "Social Mood and Financial Economics," *Journal of Behavioral Finance* 6(2005): 144–160.

15. Jędrzej Białkowski, Ahmad etebari, and Tomasz Piortr Wisniewski, "Fast Profits: Investor Sentiment and Stock Returns during Ramadan," *Journal of Banking and Finance* 36(2012): 835–845.

16. For a discussion of closed-end discounts, see Charles Lee, Andrei Shleifer, and Richard Thaler, "Investor Sentiment and the Closed-End Fund Puzzle," *Journal of Finance* 46(1991): 75–109. For a discussion of IPOs, see Roger Ibbotson, Jody Sindelar, and Jay Ritter, "The Market's Problems with the Pricing of Initial Public Offerings," *Journal of Applied Corporate Finance* 7(1994): 66–74.

17. Malcolm Baker and Jeffrey Wurgler, "Investor Sentiment and the Cross-Section of Stock Returns," *Journal of Finance* 61(2006): 1645–1680.

18. Robert Sobel, *The Big Board: A History of the New York Stock Market* (New York: Free Press, 1965).

19. Alok Kumar, "Who Gambles in the Stock Market," *Journal of Finance* 64(2009): 1889–1933.

20. Daniel Dorn and Paul Sengmeuller, "Trading as Entertainment?" *Management Science* 55(2009): 591–603.

21. Mark Grinblatt and Matti Keloharju, "Sensation Seeking, Overconfidence, and Trading Activity," *Journal of Finance* 64(2009): 549–578.

Self-Control and Decision Making

*Three years of losses often turn investors with
30-year horizons into investors with 3-year horizons;
they want out.*

KENNETH FISHER AND MEIR STATMAN[1]

A common adage on Wall Street is that the markets are motivated by two emotions: fear and greed. Indeed, this book suggests that investors are affected by these emotions. However, acting on these emotions is rarely the wise move. The decision that benefits investors over the long term is usually made in the absence of strong emotions. In fact, investors face a lifelong struggle between decisions that make the present more enjoyable and ones that make the future more enjoyable. Many decisions require balancing this trade-off. "Do I read this chapter now or later?" "Do I purchase a new stereo or invest the money for the future?"

Richard Thaler and Hersh Shefrin describe the self-control problem as the interaction between a person's two selves: the planner and the doer.[2] The doer wishes to consume now instead of later and procrastinates on unpleasant tasks. The planner wishes to save for later consumption and complete unpleasant tasks now. This conflict between desire and willpower occurs because people are influenced by long-term rational concerns and by more short-term emotional factors.

Fortunately, people recognize the fact that they are susceptible to weak willpower and spur-of-the-moment decisions. Our society is full of examples of people who recognize that they need help with self-control. Common examples are those who utilize weight-loss clinics, Alcoholics Anonymous, Narcotics Anonymous, and similar organizations.

SHORT-TERM VERSUS LONG-TERM FOCUS

People like to receive rewards early and put off unpleasant tasks. However, this attitude depends on the circumstances. Consider the following example.[3] If people are asked on February 1 whether they would prefer to do seven hours of an unpleasant task on April 1 or eight hours of the unpleasant task on April 15, people will say they would prefer to do the lesser amount of work on April 1. However, if given the same choice on the morning of April 1, most people will decide to delay the work until April 15, even though it means doing more total work. When making decisions involving the present, people often procrastinate, even when it results in more work later.

This attitude also can affect investment decisions. For example, most people would rather get $50 immediately than $100 in two years, forgoing a 41 percent annual return. Alternatively, almost no one prefers $50 in four years to $100 in six years even though this is the same choice, albeit four years into the future.[4] People seem to view the present differently from how they view the future. This leads to strong desire and weak willpower.

CONTROLLING YOURSELF

Most people want to maintain self-control and implement decisions that provide benefits over the long term. However, they often recognize that their desire is stronger than their willpower; therefore, people use many techniques to help strengthen their willpower. I categorize these techniques into two groups: rules of thumb and environment control.[5] These techniques help people reduce desire and increase willpower.

People implement rules of thumb to control their behavior. They rationally create these rules in the absence of emotions during times when willpower is high. During situations filled with high emotion and desire, people rely on these rules to remind them how to exert willpower. Consider these common rules:

- People control spending by—fighting the urge to splurge.
- Recovering alcoholics drink—not one drop.
- Retired people control spending by the rule—don't touch the principal.
- Employees contribute to their 401(k) plans by the rule—save much, don't touch.
- Investors try to control trading behavior with—buy low, sell high.
- Investors try to maintain a long-term perspective during bear markets with—stay the course.

People also control their environment to improve willpower. Common ways to control the environment are to remove desired objects from the area or avoid situations that are likely to cause self-control problems. Common examples include the following:

- People on a diet do not keep cookies in the house.
- Gambling addicts avoid going to Las Vegas.
- People who are always late set their watches a few minutes fast.
- People who have trouble getting out of bed place the alarm clock across the room to force themselves to get up.

People are often willing to incur costs in order to maintain self-control. For example, professional athletes earn the vast majority of their income during a short time period. After earning millions of dollars, some end up bankrupt because they were unable to control their desire to spend. To improve willpower, some athletes hire agents to impose limits on their consumption.

As another example, consider the average smoker. Most smokers recognize that they should not smoke too much (or at all). In order to limit their smoking, most smokers buy cigarettes by the pack. Purchasing cigarettes by the carton is much cheaper; however, the easiest way to control the number of cigarettes smoked is to control the number available. Although this technique is more expensive, smokers are willing to pay the extra cost in order to control their environment in the pursuit of stronger willpower.

SAVING AND SELF-CONTROL

Saving for retirement is difficult because it requires self-control. In 1971, 51 percent of retirees had no income from financial assets. Only 22 percent of the retirees earned investment income that amounted to more than 20 percent of their total income. Most retirees succumbed to the desire for current consumption during their peak earning years and procrastinated when it came to saving for the future.[6]

People find it psychologically easier to save from a lump-sum payment than from regular income.[7] Consider two people who each earn $25,000 per year. The first earns the $25,000 as 12 monthly payments. The second person earns $20,000 in 12 monthly payments and then receives a $5,000 bonus paid all at once. Assuming that both wage earners incur the equivalent amount in expenses, they should save the same amount for retirement. However, it is more likely that the person with the bonus will save more. Coming up with the disposable income to save is easier with a lump-sum payment (or cash windfall). Saving money from a monthly salary requires much more self-control.[8] This might be why the savings rate of countries like Japan is higher than that of the United States. A higher percentage of income in Japan is from the year-end bonus. However, a simple environmental control of automatic payroll deduction or an automatic investment plan can make saving easier.

This also explains people's propensity for giving interest-free loans to the government; that is, most people overpay their taxes throughout the year and then receive a tax refund in the spring. In 1996, approximately 76 percent of individual taxpayers overpaid their taxes an aggregate of $117 billion. That is a lot of forgone interest.

People can easily adjust their withholding rate and retain more of their income during the year. However, many prefer to overpay. In an experiment using MBA students and a case of a hypothetical wager earner, 43 percent of the 132 students chose to pay more than the minimum required quarterly tax payment.[9] People recognize that a $50 increase in their monthly income is likely to be spent. They know they are more likely to save the equivalent, a $600 refund.

401(K) AND IRA PLANS

The IRA (Individual Retirement Account) and the corporate 401(k) pension plans are two savings innovations that have helped people save and invest for the future. These plans are simple to implement and provide an immediate tax reduction. In addition, the large penalties for early withdrawal add the incentive needed to keep the money invested for retirement. Most people who invest in an IRA or a 401(k) plan contribute again the following year;[10] that is, they form a habit to help their willpower.

It is clearly rational to contribute to an IRA. The investment earnings in an IRA grow tax deferred because no income or capital gains taxes are paid on the profits each year. Instead, income taxes are paid on the money that is withdrawn from the IRA during retirement. Therefore, it is best to contribute the money to the IRA as soon as possible to let it grow tax deferred for as long as possible. To get the tax deduction for the 2013 tax year, you should contribute on January 1, 2013, to get the maximum time benefit of the money growing. However, people do not have the self-control to invest early in the year. The tax laws allow contributions made as late as April 15, 2014, to count as a 2013 tax-year IRA. Indeed, most taxpayers who contribute to an IRA will not contribute until 2014 for their 2013 IRA.[11] They need the deadline to exert self-control.

Contributing to your 401(k) plan is also considered the smart thing to do. However, since the inception of the 401(k), the most difficult aspect for plan administrators has been getting employees to begin contributing because people procrastinate. The more important the decision is, the more likely people are to procrastinate.[12] Employees often believe they can make a better decision if they just take a little more time to analyze the choices. The continuous delay costs the employee the two most important factors in building a retirement nest egg: time and invested capital.

The problem has gotten worse because companies have been increasing the number of options available in their 401(k) plans. These plans started with three or four choices (typically, company stock, money market, bond fund, and stock fund). However, many plans now adopt mutual fund families with hundreds of different funds to select from. Having more options available induces more procrastination. In order to help employees improve their self-control, some companies now automatically sign up employees for contributions when they are first hired. That way, although the employee procrastinates on how to change the automatic contribution defaults, he or she is still contributing and investing.

SELF-CONTROL AND DIVIDENDS

A long-standing puzzle in traditional finance has been why individuals have a strong preference for cash dividends. This is especially puzzling considering that dividend income is taxed at a higher marginal rate than capital gains.

Consider the example demonstrated in Table 11.1. An investor owns 1,000 shares of a $100 stock for a total value of $100,000. If the stock pays a 1 percent dividend, then the investor receives $1,000, and the stock price falls to $99 per share. The 1,000 shares are now worth $99,000 because the investment paid out 1 percent of its value. The decrease in the stock price is the amount of the dividend paid. However, if the investor owes 20 percent in dividend tax, he keeps only $800 after taxes. In sum, the investor ends up with $800 in cash and stock worth $99,000.

Now consider the alternative. Assume that the stock does not pay a dividend. If the investor wants some cash, he must create his own dividend by selling 10 shares at $100 per share to receive the $1,000 in proceeds. This is called a *homemade dividend*. The investor is now left with 990 shares of a stock worth $100 each for a total of $99,000. If the stock sold has no capital gains liability, then the investor owes no taxes and keeps the entire $1,000 in cash. Note that the investor is better off creating his own dividend. If the stock had a cost basis of $50 per share and capital gains are taxed at 20 percent, then $100 is owed in taxes. The investor is still better off making his own dividends.

TABLE 11.1   Real Dividends Versus Homemade Dividends

	Real Dividend	Homemade Dividend
Starting Number of Shares Owned	1,000	1,000
Beginning Price per Share	$100	$100
Beginning Stock Value	$100,000	$100,000
Per-Share Dividend	$1	$0
Pretax Dividend Income	$1,000	
Dividend by Selling Ten Shares		
Selling Shares Pretax Income		$1,000
Ending Number of Shares	1,000	990
Price per Share	$99	$100
Ending Stock Value	$99,000	$99,000
Taxes		
Dividend Tax (20% Rate)	$200	$0
Capital Gains Tax (20% Rate, 50% Gain)	$0	$100
After-Tax Income	$800	$900

The investor who wishes to maximize wealth and cash flow should seek income through homemade dividends rather than cash dividends. However, people generally prefer cash dividends. This behavior is irrational in traditional finance but can be explained by investor psychology.

Mental accounting causes investors to separate investments into different mental accounts. In investing for the income mental account, investors buy high-dividend stocks, bonds, and annuities. A different mental account is used for capital gains.

These mental accounts are especially useful for investors who need to exert self-control. Retired people may recognize that their wealth needs to outlive themselves; that is, they don't want to outlive their money. Because they might be tempted to spend too much money, they enact a common rule of thumb to help with self-control: never touch the principal. This rule is a helpful reminder to avoid overspending. However, it can also inhibit the kind of creative thinking that increases income, such as the use of homemade dividends.

BEATING THE BIASES

Many biases have been discussed in this book. This section suggests strategies for overcoming the psychological biases.

Strategy 1: Understand the Biases

This is the purpose of the previous chapters of this book. Recognizing the biases in yourself and in others is an important step in avoiding them.

Strategy 2: Know Why You Are Investing

Many investors largely overlook this simple step of the investing process. Most people have only some vague notion of their investment goals. "I want a lot of money so I can travel abroad when I retire." "I want to make the money to send my kids to college." Sometimes people think of vague goals in a negative form. "I don't want to be poor when I retire." These vague notions do little to provide investment direction, nor do they help you avoid the psychological biases that inhibit good decision making.

Establishing specific goals and ways to meet them is important. Instead of a vague notion of wanting to travel after retirement, define what that means and how much money it will require. For example,

---

A minimum of $75,000 of income per year in retirement would allow me to make two international trips per year. I will receive $20,000 per year in Social Security and retirement benefits, so I need $55,000 in investment income. Investment earnings from $800,000 would generate the desired income. I want to retire in 10 years.

Having specific goals gives you many advantages. For example, by keeping your eye on the reason for investing, you will focus on the long term and "the big picture," be able to monitor and measure your progress, and be able to determine whether your behavior matches your goals.

Strategy 3: Have Quantitative Investment Criteria

Having a set of quantitative investment criteria allows you to avoid investing on emotion, rumor, stories, and other psychologically based biases. This is important because investors seem to be attracted to attention-grabbing information like advertising. Mutual funds that advertise more than other funds receive more new money flow from investors. However, their annual expenses are higher because of the 12B-1 fee charged to fund shareholders for advertising.[13] So, while investors are attracted to funds that advertise, they are simultaneously picking higher expense funds, which is negatively related to performance.

Before buying a stock or mutual fund, compare its characteristics to your criteria. If it doesn't meet your criteria, don't invest in it.

Consider the Klondike Investment Club of Buffalo, Wyoming, discussed in Chapter 9. Their number one ranking stems in part from the fact that they make buying decisions based only on an acceptable research report. Their criteria keep them from falling prey to their psychological biases. On the other hand, the California Investors Club's lack of success is partially due to their lack of criteria. Their decision process leads to buying decisions that are ultimately controlled by emotion.

Even though quantitative criteria are used, qualitative information also can be important. Information about the quality of the firm's management or the types of new products under development can be useful. If a stock meets your quantitative criteria, then you can examine these qualitative factors.

Strategy 4: Diversify

It is not likely that you will diversify in a manner suggested by modern portfolio theory as discussed in Chapter 6. However, if you keep some simple diversification rules in mind, you can do well.

- *Diversify by owning many different types of stocks.* You can be reasonably well diversified with 15 stocks that are from different industries and are of different-sized companies. One diversified mutual fund would accomplish this goal, too. However, a portfolio of 50 technology stocks is not a diversified portfolio; neither is one that includes five technology mutual funds.
- *Own very little of the firm you work for.* You already have your human capital invested in the firm; that is, your income is dependent on the company. Therefore, diversify your "whole self" by avoiding the company in your investments.
- *Invest in bonds, too.* A diversified portfolio should include some bonds or bond mutual funds.

Diversifying in this way helps investors avoid tragic losses that can truly affect their lives. In addition, diversification is a shield against the psychological biases of attachment and familiarity.

Strategy 5: Control Your Investing Environment

If you are on a diet, you should not leave a dish of M&M candies on the table. Similarly, if you want to overcome your psychological investment biases, you should control your investment environment.

So many people are frequently checking their stocks at work that companies are limiting Internet access to employees so they are not distracted. To control your environment, you need to limit the activities that magnify your psychological biases. Here are some ways to help you control your environment:

- *Check your stocks once per month.* By checking your stocks once per month instead of once per hour, the behavioral reactions of snakebite, seeking pride, and playing with the house's money will be inhibited.
- *Make trades only once per month and on the same day of the month.* Pick one day of the month, such as the fifteenth, and place buy-and-sell trades only on that day. This will help you avoid the misconception that speed is important. Speed is important only if you want to chase a stock on a rumor and get into it just before its bubble bursts. On the other hand, trading once per month helps overcome overconfidence trading.
- *Review your portfolio annually to see how it lines up with your specific goals.* When you review your portfolio, keep in mind the psychological biases of status quo, endowment, representativeness, and familiarity. Does each security in your portfolio contribute to meeting your investment goals and maintaining diversification? Keep records so that you can overcome cognitive dissonance and other memory biases.

ADDITIONAL RULES OF THUMB

Although many people understand these self-help concepts, they still fail to exert the effort needed to implement them. Instead, they attempt to cope by adopting simple heuristics (or rules of thumb).[14] Consider implementing these rules to shield yourself from your own psychological biases:

1. Avoid stocks that are selling for less than $5 per share. Most investment scams are conducted in penny stocks.
2. Chat rooms and message boards are for entertainment purposes only. It is on these boards that your overconfidence is fostered, familiarity is magnified, and artificial "social consensus" is formed.
3. Before you place a trade on a stock that does not meet your criteria, remember that it is unlikely that you know more than the market. Investing outside of your criteria implies that you have some informational advantage over others. Are you sure you know more?
4. Strive to earn the market return. Most active trading is motivated by the desire to earn a higher return than everyone else. The strategies for earning a higher return usually foster psychological biases and ultimately contribute to lower returns. However, the strategies for earning the market return, like fully diversifying, are successful because they inhibit your biases.
5. Review the psychological biases annually. This action will reinforce the first strategy of the chapter.

Successful investing is more than just knowing all about stocks. Indeed, understanding yourself is equally important. "Knowledgeable" investors frequently fail because they allow their psychological biases to control their decisions. This chapter illustrates the self-control problem and proposes some strategies for overcoming the psychological biases.

MAYBE AN ADVISOR IS NEEDED?

As this book has illustrated, there are many biases, emotions, and cognitive errors that lead people to make serious investment mistakes. These problems are hard to control, especially for the "part-time" investor. Would a financial advisor help?

There are several issues with using a financial advisor. First, advisors are people too and may also suffer from many of these same psychological biases. Second, people tend to shy away from advisors who charge a fee and then give unbiased advice. I'll call this the Suze Orman effect. But financial advisors need to earn a living and get paid for their advice, so many must then get compensated by earning sales charges when they put clients in mutual funds that charge sales loads. This allows for potential conflicts of interest for the advisors.[15] Do they recommend investments that are best for their clients or that give them the most compensation? Lastly, many investors don't seem to believe that advisors will provide useful advice.

Indeed, scholars recently tested that last sentence. They offered free and unbiased financial advice to clients of one of the largest brokerages in Germany.[16] The advice focused on improving portfolio efficiency through better diversification and it was generated from a mean-variance optimizer targeted to the client's level of risk aversion. The products recommended were mostly combinations of exchange-traded funds and the brokerage agreed to waive commissions for any client following the advice. A total of 8,195 customers were offered the free advice. Only 5 percent, or 385, people accepted the offer to hear the advice. The advice offered these 385 was good. It recommended lower allocations to German stocks (home bias) and greater investment in foreign stocks and other asset classes. The researchers followed the recommended portfolios and the actual investor portfolios after the recommendation was made. The post advice average return was 24.8 percent for the recommended portfolios versus 21.2 percent for the actual portfolios. The standard deviation was only 9.6 percent for the recommendations versus 15.0 percent. However, of the 385 people who accepted the offer and heard the advice, only 125 actually took some part of the advice. Clearly, many people are simply not interested in hearing or taking professional financial advice.

USING BIASES FOR GOOD

This book has shown that people don't often know their own preferences. Even when they do, their preferences are often unclear and ill-formed. Their decisions are influenced by cognitive errors, framing effects, mental shortcuts, social influences, and other psychological biases. When people are given the freedom of choice in financial decisions, they often choose badly. Should the government, corporations, and other institutions choose for them?

This is a question of ideology. Libertarians advocate the maximization of individual liberty, thus they value the freedom of choice. On the other hand, paternalism is the attitude that an authoritative figurehead should make decisions on behalf of others for their own good. Thus, Richard Thaler and Cass Sunstein's promotion of libertarian paternalism seems like an oxymoron. In their book, *Nudge*, they argue that private and public institutions should attempt to guide people's decisions and behavior in a direction that will improve their own welfare.[17] That is, peoples' choices should be deliberately framed in a manner that steers them to making choices that will make them better off. Yet in the end, each person is free to choose. For example, health-care options can be framed in a manner that leads to healthier lifestyles. Below are two examples of savings programs that are designed to exploit behavioral biases for the good of the person.

Save More Tomorrow

Most discussions of psychological biases, including those in this book, focus on how the biases are problems for investors and how they can be overcome. However, by reorganizing the investment process, some biases can be used to help investors. For example, instead of setting up a 401(k) plan process where social and psychological influences inhibit employees from contributing, it might be better to set up the process in ways such that the influences encourage employees to contribute.

The status quo bias causes employees to procrastinate in making their retirement plan decisions. Indeed, many procrastinate so long that they never participate in the plan. Instead of requiring the new employee to take action to enroll, enroll the employee automatically and require the person to take action to disenroll.[18] Instead of exerting an effort to start the participation, employees participate automatically. Those not wishing to participate must make the effort to disenroll. An automatic enrollment policy in a 401(k) savings plan results in substantially more employees participating in the pension plan, although most just stay at the default level of contribution and asset allocation. One problem with this approach is that some of the employees would have participated without the automatic enrollment. In addition, they would have contributed a higher amount and chosen a more aggressive asset allocation than the default money market fund, but they do not change the default allocation because of the status quo bias. Therefore, this automatic enrollment of employees helps many but might harm some.

Richard Thaler and Shlomo Benartzi proposed a four-step approach that they call Save More Tomorrow (SMT) that overcomes several psychological biases.[19] They suggested that employees who are not contributing to their 401(k) plan can begin to do so by agreeing to the following plan. First, the employee is asked to agree to the plan well in advance; that is, the decision does not have any immediate ramifications. Second, the plan starts by having the employee agree to begin contributing at his or her next pay raise with a small contribution rate, such as 2 percent. By combining a pay raise with the contribution, the employee still sees a small increase in pay but also begins contributing.

Third, the employee agrees to increase the contribution rate at each pay raise until a preset maximum level is reached. Fourth, the employee can opt out of the plan at any time. Although the hope is that employees will not opt out, the ability to do so makes them more comfortable about joining the plan. The SMT plan requires the employees to make decisions far in advance, and then the status quo bias works to their advantage because they do not take the option of opting out of the plan.

This plan was tested at a midsize manufacturing company whose savings participation rate was low. The 315 employees had an average savings rate of 4.4 percent of their earnings. They were asked to increase their contribution by 5 percent. Those employees who claimed they could not contribute the 5 percent were offered the SMT program. The program was made available to 207 employees, and 162 employees agreed to join. These employees had a low savings rate of 3.5 percent, on average. The 153 employees who did not join the SMT plan either did nothing or made a one-time increase in their savings rate. On average, the people who did not adopt the SMT plan had a savings rate of 5.3 percent. The effect of joining the plan was dramatic. After three pay raises, those who had joined the SMT plan had increased their savings rate from 3.5 to 11.6 percent. Those who did not join the SMT plan increased their savings rate from 5.3 to only 7.5 percent. The dramatic increase in the savings rate associated with the SMT plan was beneficial to those employees because they began saving more for their retirement. It was also beneficial to the managers of the firm because the company was being constrained by the antidiscrimination rules of the U.S. Department of Labor. Those rules restrict the proportion of retirement contributions that can be made by the higher-income employees when the lower-paid employees have low contribution rates.

The challenge for people in the financial industry is to develop more programs in which people's own psychological biases help them make good decisions instead of bad ones.

Save and Win

Another such program has been tried to help lower-income households to save more. Low-income families in the United States play lotteries, and they believe that they are more likely to become rich from lotteries than from saving. Thus, to encourage more savers and savings, consider a savings product that has a lottery prize drawing. These lottery-linked deposit accounts use each savings deposit (or bond purchased) as a "buy-in" to win lottery prizes selected frequently. The excitement of gambling draws people to start saving. The savers earn a slightly lower interest rate than they could obtain elsewhere. The difference between what they could obtain and what they get is used for the lottery prizes periodically awarded. This structure appeals to loss-adverse investors. They have the safety of the savings account and the excitement of the potential to win a lottery.[20]

Although these programs have existed for centuries internationally, the longest running program may be the Premium Bond in Britain, started in 1956. The bonds require a £100 minimum purchase and make the purchaser eligible for monthly prize drawings. The excitement of gambling is maintained as more than 1 million prizes are given at each drawing, from two £1 million prizes to more than a million £50 prizes. Over £30 billion of savings are held in Premium Bonds by one-quarter of British households. Programs in Central and South America give away cars and equivalent prizes daily with larger lotteries drawn monthly. The Million-a-Month-Account program was started by First National Bank in South Africa in 2005.

Recently, a program called "Save to Win" was started by the D2D Fund in Michigan and implemented through several credit unions. Each $25 deposit into a savings account gives a chance to win (up to 10 chances) monthly cash prizes (cash, gift cards, laptops, etc.) and accumulates for chances to win the annual $100,000 grand prize. Time will tell how successful this program will be in promoting saving. A sum of $90 billion is spent gambling in the United States each year; if only a small fraction of that is done through lottery-linked savings accounts, those individuals would be much better off!

Summary

People face a lifelong struggle between decisions that make life more enjoyable today and ones that improve life in the future. Saving and education are good examples. Self-control helps us to focus on the long-term in order to tip the balance towards the future. Self-control is also needed to reduce our susceptibility to psychological biases. The first step is to understand the biases. Then control the investment processes by knowing why you are investing, have specific investment criteria, and being sure to diversify.

Lastly, control your environment. Unbiased financial advisors can help, but few investors seem to value the advice.

Institutions, financial firms, and governments are starting to learn how to frame decisions in such a way that people's psychological biases help them, instead of hurt them. We can create investment processes that improve savings (like Save to Win) and retirement plan investing (like Save More Tomorrow).

Questions

1. How can rules of thumb be used to avoid making psychological bias-induced errors? Give examples.
2. What biases might be overcome by having quantitative criteria?
3. What biases might be overcome by reviewing one's stocks and portfolio infrequently?
4. What does libertarian paternalism refer to?

Notes

1. Kenneth Fisher and Meir Statman, "A Behavioral Framework for Time Diversification," *Financial Analysts Journal* (May/June 1999): 92.

2. This discussion is from Richard Thaler and Hersh Shefrin, "An Economic Theory of Self-Control," *Journal of Political Economy* 89(1981): 392–406.

3. This example is proposed in Ted O'Donoghue and Matthew Rabin, "Doing It Now or Later," *American Economic Review* 89(1999): 103–124.

4. George Ainsle, "Derivation of 'Rational' Economic Behavior from Hyperbolic Discount Curves," *American Economic Review* 81(1991): 334–340.

5. These ideas are explored in Richard Thaler and Hersh Shefrin, "An Economic Theory of Self-Control," *Journal of Political Economy* 89(1981): 392–406 and Stephen Hoch and George Loewenstein, "Time-Inconsistent Preferences and Consumer Self-Control," *Journal of Consumer Research* 17(1991): 492–507.

6. George Akerlof, "Procrastination and Obedience," *American Economic Review* 81(1991): 1–19.

7. Richard Thaler, "Psychology and Savings Policies," *American Economic Review* 84(1994): 186–192.

8. Richard Thaler and Hersh Shefrin, "An Economic Theory of Self-Control," *Journal of Political Economy* 89(1981): 392–406.

9. Benjamin Ayers, Steven Kachelmeister, and John Robinson, "Why Do People Give Interest-Free Loans to the Government? An Experimental Study of Interim Tax Payments," *Journal of the American Taxation Association* 21(1999): 55–74.

10. Richard Thaler, "Psychology and Savings Policies," *American Economic Review* 84(1994): 186–192.

11. Hersh Shefrin and Richard Thaler, "Mental Accounting, Saving, and Self-Control," in *Choice over Time*, ed. George Loewenstein and Jon Elster (New York: Russell Sage Foundation, 1992).

12. This discussion is adapted from Ted O'Donoghue and Matthew Rabin, "Choice and Procrastination," *Quarterly Journal of Economics* 116(2001): 121–160.

13. See Brad Barber, Terrance Odean, and Lu Zheng, "Out of Sight, Out of Mind: The Effects of Expenses on Mutual Fund Flows,"*Journal of Business,* 78(2005): 2095–2119 and Prem Jain and Joanna Wu, "Truth in Mutual Fund Advertising: Evidence on Future Performance and Fund Flows," *Journal of Finance* 55(2000): 937–958.

14. Shlomo Benartzi and Richard Thaler, "Heuristics and Biases in Retirement Savings Behavior," *Journal of Economic Perspectives* 21(2007): 81–104.

15. See both Patrick Bolton, Xavier Freixas, and Joel Shapiro, "Conflicts of Interest, Information Provision, and Compensation in the Financial Services Industry," *Journal of Financial Economics* 85(2007): 297–330 and Neal M. Stoughton, Youchang Wu, and Josef Zechner, "Intermediated Investment Management," *Journal of Finance* 66(2011): 947–980.

16. Utpal Bhattacharya, Andreas Hackethal, Simon Kaesler, Benjamin Loos, and Steffen Meyer, "Is Unbiased Financial Advice to Retail Investors Sufficient? Answers from a Large Field Study," *Review of Financial Studies* 25(2012): 975–1032.

17. Also see Cass Sunstein and Richard Thaler, "Libertarian Paternalism Is Not an Oxymoron," *The University of Chicago Law Review* 70(2003): 1159–1202.

18. Brigitte Madrian and Dennis Shea, "The Power of Suggestion: Inertia in 401(k) Participation and Savings Behavior," *Quarterly Journal of Economics* 116(2001): 1149–1187.

19. Richard Thaler and Shlomo Benartzi, "Save More Tomorrow: Using Behavioral Economics to Increase Employee Savings," *Journal of Political Economy* 112(2004): S164–S187.

20. See the following: Peter Tufano, "Saving Whilst Gambling: An Empirical Analysis of UK Premium Bonds," *American Economic Review* 98(2008): 321–326; Mauro Guillen and Adrian Tschoegl, "Banking on Gambling: Banks and Lottery-Linked Deposit Accounts," *Journal of Financial Services Research* 21(2002): 219–231; and Peter Tufano and Daniel Schneider, "Using Financial Innovation to Support Savers: From Coercion to Excitement," in *Access, Assets and Poverty*, ed. Rebecca Blank and Michael Barr (New York: Russell Sage, 2008).

Psychology in the Mortgage Crisis

There is a great deal of interesting behaviors that helped set the stage for the financial crisis. The financial crisis started in the mortgage industry and eventually transmitted to banking and even governments. This chapter examines the cognitive errors at work in several different aspects of the crisis, starting with the subprime mortgage contracts.[1] The topics then progress to the U.S. government, banks, and investors.

Chapter 11 describes several programs cleverly designed to use peoples' own psychological biases to benefit themselves through better saving behavior. But this is a double-edged sword. Programs can also be designed to exploit people through their cognitive errors. Specifically, predatory subprime lenders designed products and marketing programs to trick borrowers by hiding important characteristics of contracts through taking advantage of people's tendency to focus on a couple of salient dimensions, like the initial closing cost and initial monthly payments.

This chapter describes these exploitations, as well as the social norms of debt contracts around the financial crisis.

MORTGAGE INDUSTRY

Real estate always goes up, right? This was the experience of many people in the 1990s and through 2006, as shown in Figure 12.1 Housing prices increased by 50 percent from 1991 to 2001, and the rise was even larger in many cities and states. Prices doubled from 2001 to 2006. Investor returns were even bigger

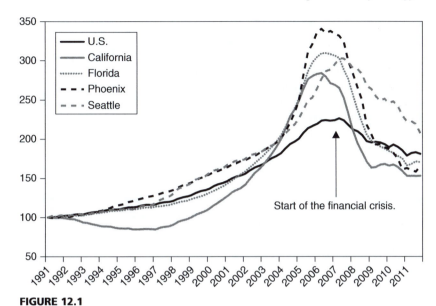

FIGURE 12.1

because real estate investors usually use a high degree of financial leverage. Robert Shiller told the Federal Reserve at the annual Jackson Hole conference that he believed the real estate bubble could not be explained by fundamentals.[2] He blamed the psychology behind a social epidemic of the view that housing was an investment, and a speculative one at that.

People seemed to suffer from groupthink about real estate. Groupthink occurs when members of a group minimize conflict to the common assumptions by reaching consensus without critically testing and analyzing them.[3] Society seemed to assume that housing prices don't fall. When a particular type of investing becomes highly popular, watch out! Consider that Real Estate TV, a U.K.-based property television channel that broadcasted 24 hours a day, was launched in October 2004. A whole channel devoted to real estate! The next year in the United States, the first episode of *Flip That House* aired on July 14, 2005. Each episode featured a person who recently bought a house and was then trying to profitably and quickly resell (or "flip") it. Real estate became thought of as a speculative and tradable asset for some people, instead of an investment. This phenomenon was not just localized to the United States. Massive real estate bubbles also occurred in the countries of Australia, Canada, China, France, India, Ireland, Italy, Korea, Russia, Spain, and the United Kingdom.

Subprime Mortgages

Many people blame the financial crisis on the financial engineering that created the mortgage-related derivative securities. Those products read like alphabet soup, such as MBS, ABSs, CDOs, and CDS. These securities became even more risky when the underlying mortgages were subprime. There were many problems in the subprime mortgage industry that can be blamed on many participants.[4] For example, aggressive mortgage lenders did not worry about repayment risk because the institutions that bought the loans for the securitizing process didn't seem to be concerned. Real estate appraisers marked up house values to accommodate the loan to value ratios needed for the sales. Those institutions that securitized the debt wanted higher yields and believed that the diversification effect in their loan pools would mitigate much of the credit risk of subprime borrowers.

Although there were many participants in the subprime mortgage industry, this section focuses on the psychology around the borrowers. The term *subprime* refers to the category of loans for people with higher credit risk, as typically measured by the FICO credit score. Because of the higher default risks, lenders charge subprime borrowers higher interest rates. Payday loans are an extreme form of subprime lending. The subprime mortgage contract became increasingly complex and by 2007, it had evolved into time bombs for the borrowers. They had large fees and temporarily low monthly payments that reset to high payments and interest rates. Why did people accept the bad loans? Consider how the subprime industry exploited their psychological biases.

Two major psychological problems are as follows: (1) People have difficulty processing complex, multidimensional contracts and (2) people often underestimate future costs. Information overload is a potential cognitive problem for many people. We tend to focus on just a few salient attributes on which to base our decision when overwhelmed with a lot of complex information. Note that decisions involving higher complexity and emotional stress reduce the number of things we focus on. Emotional stress includes fear, anger, embarrassment, annoyance, and frustration. Financial decision mistakes are more widespread for the elderly.[5] Thus, the elderly who were emotionally distressed were the primary targets of exploitation.

People linearize functions containing exponential terms, like the interest rate compounding equations. This causes an underestimate of future costs.[6] That is, people underestimate the costs of borrowing and the future value of savings. This effect is called the *exponential growth bias*. In addition, people tend to be optimistic about their future ability to pay loans or save for the future.

Mortgage originators played into those biases by making contracts complex with more deferred costs.[7] A high degree of complexity forces the borrower to focus on just a few salient items that can be manipulated so that they underestimate the total costs. What salient dimension do they focus on? Potential candidates are present closing fees, interest rate, monthly mortgage payment, total cost over the life of the loan, etc. For example, consider the straight forward, traditional, 30-year, fixed rate mortgage. Borrowers could focus on the two salient cost measures, monthly payment and amount of money down, and be able to understand the mortgage. But the new subprime mortgages allow for financing the closing costs by adding them to the loan principle, thus lowering the amount of money down needed. In addition, a low teaser rate caused the initial monthly payment to be artificially low and temporary. Therefore, when a borrower focuses on the monthly payment and initial closing payment, these loans appear cheap. But they are actually very costly. The magnitude of the points is hidden by adding them to the loan balance. The borrower also then pays finance fees through the life of the loan. Also, the low teaser rate resets in a couple of years to a very high rate, causing the monthly payment to double or increase even more. Additional increases in complexity come with balloon payments and negative amortization, which decrease the monthly payment while lowering the long term cost. These contracts required many dozens of pages of legal jargon. All of these variations and complexity make choosing an optimal contract difficult for even knowledgeable borrowers.

Subprime lenders made up many official-sounding origination fees, as many as 15 fees, that added up to thousands of dollars and as much as 20 percent of the loan amount. Note that this bundling together of many small fees exploits an aspect of prospect theory. Recall from prospect theory that people exhibit a diminishing sensitivity to losses. In other words, we feel bad about a $2,000 loss, or cost. We feel worse about a $4,000 loss. But even though the $4,000 loss is twice the $2,000 loss, we do not feel twice as bad about it. Thus, it is more likely that the loan applicant will agree to pay all the fees if they are bundled together rather than addressed individually.

These fees were added to the loan balance, which helps to hide their total. This would increase the monthly payment due to paying interest and principle on the fees. However, the subprime mortgages evolved in ways that minimized initial monthly payments. For example, some interest only and payment–option adjustable rate mortgages (ARMs) had zero, or even negative, amortization during the first few years. Thus, brokers were able to earn high fees originating these mortgages because the costs were hidden through the design of highly salient attributes of low initial costs (as in low closing cost and initial monthly payments). The actual high costs of the loans were present in the less salient dimensions that impacted future costs. Unfortunately, many of these borrowers would experience financial distress because of the mortgage structure. The delinquency rate for these subprime mortgages was 10 percent in 2001 and subsequently climbed to nearly 40 percent in 2008.[8]

An additional complication is that people have trouble understanding percentages in the context of compounding. For example, people frame interest rates in the mental scale of 0 percent to 100 percent. On that scale, the difference between 10 percent and 10.8 percent seems small. So mortgage brokers can add small percentages to the rate without strong objections. But an increase from 10 percent to 10.8 percent would increase the monthly payment in a 30-year mortgage by nearly 7 percent. An additional problem with scaling occurs from the magnitude effect bias. People frequently fail to appreciate the difference between large values. For example, the difference between 3,000 and 7,000 seems large, but the difference between 203,000 and 207,000 does not. Thus, adding extra closing costs to the total loan principle goes unnoticed by most borrowers.

Emotional Stress and Frame Manipulation

The people who are most susceptible to these manipulated frames are those people who have trouble thinking through the reframing of the costs. Thus, anyone with a low level of financial literacy, the elderly, and those experiencing emotional distress were targets.[9] For example, these subprime loans were prominent in lower-income neighborhoods, where people had less access to financial education. These neighborhoods are disproportionately African American and Latino. This is the reverse of the "redlining" that banks were accused of 40 years earlier, in which they refused to lend in similar neighborhoods. These neighborhoods appear to have been targeted for subprime mortgages. In addition, the elderly were often targeted because cognitive ability degrades with old age.

Predatory lenders also sought out people likely to be emotionally stressed. Stress causes a truncated reasoning process. Some of the thinking capacity of a shared person is devoted to contemplating the issues causing the stress. Thus, there is less capacity available to cope with the mortgage issues. The person feels an information overload compared to the available cognitive capacity. To deal with this overload, the person will not try to assimilate all the information, but simply focus on a few dimensions of it. This fits well with the design of the subprime mortgage contracts that lead people to the few, specifically framed, salient decision factors. Financial distress causes emotional stress. Lauren Willis concludes that "lenders and brokers search courthouse records for home loan owners facing foreclosure or tax liens and buy lists of home loan owners with overdue balances on their credit cards or medical debt."[10]

In addition, the very act of taking a subprime mortgage can lead quickly lead to financial distress and ensuing emotional stress. Predatory lenders sometimes refinanced their subprime mortgage clients several times while claiming to try to "fix" the problem—a practice referred to as mortgage flipping. In testimony before the U.S. Congress, Ms. Mary Pedelco describes how an original loan of $11,921 turned into a balance of $64,000 after the fifth flip.[11] After the sixth flip, her monthly payments were $439. Her only source of income was her $470 monthly social security payment. After the seventh flip, the house went into foreclosure. The increase in the mortgage balance was due to the new fees added into the loan at each refinance. Unfortunately, this abusive lending behavior has been too common.

Stress on all mortgage applicants is increased by rushing the document-signing process. For example, brokers would pressure the applicant to review and sign the documents of more than 40 pages in a short period of time. Emotionally distressed people also tend to make quick, impulsive decisions.

Society Cross-Subsidy

The number of subprime mortgages sold exploded from 2000 to 2006. But not everyone took a subprime mortgage. Many households acquired the traditional, 30- or 15-year, fixed rate mortgage with low interest rates and low fees. Prime and subprime mortgage products allowed brokers to separate customers by their level of sophistication.[12] The better educated and financially savvy could evaluate the high degree of complexity in the subprime mortgages and discern how costly they were. Thus, savvy households paid lower mortgage costs while the naïve households paid high costs. Given the neighborhoods in which the purposely complex subprime mortgages were predominately sold, the naïve households tended to be at the lower-income levels. Traditional mortgages were predominately sold in white, middle, and upper-income neighborhoods. The high fees paid in the poor neighborhoods, in effect, subsidized the fees paid in the upper middle class and wealthy neighborhoods.[13] The result is a cross-subsidy from the less wealthy to the wealthier.

HOUSEHOLDS IN DISTRESS

During an economic recession, many people lose their job and sometimes have to declare bankruptcy and lose a home to foreclosure. The 2007 to 2009 recession in the United States also came with an unusually large housing price decline as shown earlier. This resulted in a relatively new phenomenon; some people appeared to walk away from their homes when their mortgages had become underwater even though they were financially stable. When the value of a house declines to significantly less than the mortgage balance, it is referred to as underwater. The term *strategic default* is used if a homeowner who can continue to pay the monthly mortgage decides to walk away from a house, letting the bank foreclose, just because it is underwater.

Interestingly, in 2009, the former chairman of the Council of Economic Advisors for President Ronald Reagan and Harvard professor, Martin Feldstein, noted that about one sixth of the homes with mortgages were severely underwater with a loan-to-value ratio of 130 percent or more. He also felt that homeowners had a strong economic incentive to default when the loan-to-value rises to over 120 percent.[14] Professor Feldstein was advocating that the government work with creditors to reduce loan principles for these households. On the other hand, University of Arizona Law Professor Brent White described strategic defaults as an in-the-money option and advocated default for many situations.[15] But even though many households had strong economic incentives to strategically default, the vast majority of financially stable underwater homeowners did not default. Why?

Mortgage Default: Social Norms and Psychology

Chapter 9 illustrated how social norms influence our behavior. Professor White believes that these social norms have played a large role in keeping homeowners in severely underwater houses. The fear of a social stigma inhibits the homeowner from strategically defaulting. Financial economists Luigi Guiso, Paola Sapienza, and Luigi Zingales (GSZ) examine this issue by surveying over 6,000 people using multiple surveys from 2008 to 2010 and found that 82 percent of households viewed a strategic default as being morally wrong.[16] This perception appears widespread and thus can be considered a social norm, though they find this attitude is less prevalent for people who are angrier at the economic situation or distrust banks. Women have stronger feelings against strategic defaults. Nevertheless, if the home value dropped to be $50,000 below the loan value, 9 percent of the people claimed they would default. This rose to 23 percent if the home value fell to $100,000 below the loan value. These numbers are likely understated because people generally don't admit to a socially undesirable action.

GSZ also try to assess the proportion of all mortgage defaults that were by households that were not having significant cash flow problems but were underwater. They asked their survey participants for information about people they knew who had defaulted. They estimate that 26 percent of the defaults were strategic in 2009 and this increased to 35 percent in 2010. Note that these defaults represent a small portion of the total number of underwater households. Thus, it appears that the morality social norm of debt contracts is likely contributing to many homeowners continuing to pay their mortgage on a severely underwater house. However, the stigma of foreclosure may be waning as more and more people know someone who has defaulted or declared bankruptcy.

In addition to social norms, psychological biases likely also play a role in inhibiting strategic defaults. Consider the cognitive dissonance described in Chapter 4 as a reaction to the mental distress of dealing with two conflicting ideas. A homeowner wants to believe he made a good decision to purchase the house. But recent news about house values may contradict this self-image. In order to avoid the mental distress, the cognitive process can selectively filter this new information. In other words, homeowners may simply ignore the bad news.

Government's Use of Psychology in Mortgage Social Policy

The U.S. government does not want people to strategically default on their mortgages because that just makes the housing and banking crisis worse. Indeed, the government didn't really want anyone defaulting and created several programs to help the situation. Since the moral social norms are helping to inhibit strategic defaults, policy makers want to keep the social stigma of default strong. If the moral bond weakens, more strategic defaults may occur. Foreclosures in a region allow the neighbors to better understand the process and reduce the stigma for others. As more defaults occur, it weakens the social norm and fosters more defaults. To try to fix the housing problem, the U.S. government has enacted several programs with creditors and provided first-time home buyer tax credit incentives. Information and success rates on these programs are easily found for the interested reader. But this chapter focuses on the behavioral policies that target those underwater homeowners.

Consider two types of homeowners who might default on their mortgage: those with cash flow problems and those seeking to get out from a severely underwater house. During the recession, high unemployment rates pushed many homeowners into financial distress. In addition, the subprime mortgage interest rate resets to a high rate after the initial two or three year low teaser rate period. This caused many homeowners to experience a doubling or even tripling of their monthly mortgage payment. These households suffer from cash flow problems that may ultimately force them to default on their mortgage and even declare bankruptcy. The other type of homeowner who could potentially default is the underwater household who could make the payments, but may still default because of their negative equity position. They are the would-be strategic defaulters.

The U.S. government has designed programs to help the problem cash flow households. These policy initiatives include the Make Homes Affordable program through Fannie or Freddie Mac refinancing, Hope for Homeowners from the FHA to insure the newly refinanced mortgages, and working with lenders to modify mortgage terms.

Compare these programs to the use of behavioral tactics to shame the underwater households into staying in their homes. Professor White claims that the government was using social pressure on the underwater households using rhetoric to embarrass them. For example, former Treasury Secretary Hank Paulson said to the National Association of Business Economics:[17]

> And let me emphasize, any homeowner who can afford his mortgage payment but chooses to walk away from an underwater property is simply a speculator—and one who is not honoring his obligations.

Nearly a year later, President Obama characterized homeowners as either responsible or irresponsible in his speech on foreclosure and his housing plan.[18] He characterizes some homeowners of distressed houses as being responsible:

> It begins with a young family—maybe in Mesa, or Glendale, or Tempe—or just as likely in suburban Las Vegas, Cleveland, or Miami. They save up. They search. They choose a home that feels like the perfect place to start a life. They secure a fixed-rate mortgage at a reasonable rate, make a down payment, and make their mortgage payments each month. They are as responsible as anyone could ask them to be. But then they learn that acting responsibly often isn't enough to escape this crisis.

But others are characterized as amoral:

> But I also want to be very clear about what this plan will not do: It will not rescue the unscrupulous or irresponsible by throwing good taxpayer money after bad loans. It will not help speculators who took risky bets on a rising market and bought homes not to live in but to sell. It will not help dishonest lenders who acted irresponsibly, distorting the facts and dismissing the fine print at the expense of buyers who didn't know better. And it will not reward folks who bought homes they knew from the beginning they would never be able to afford. In short, this plan will not save every home.

Always be mindful of the law of unintended consequences. Programs designed to manipulate behavior through the promotion of social stigma may create unintended consequences. People often think drastic actions are justified when they believe they have been treated unfairly. Underwater households could feel that they are being isolated and that no one is looking out for them. Thus, they feel they must look out for themselves, which could result in the decision to strategically default. In addition, many of the programs to help the cash flow problem households involved tax payer money. In that sense, potential strategic defaulters may feel that they are paying for their distressed neighbor's mortgage while being lectured about their own. This gives rise to the feeling of unfairness. We can gain some insight into this issue from the GSZ surveys. They found that people who support the strong moral commitment in the debt contract tend not to support taxpayer-supported programs that help people who have defaulted. Therefore, the more that the government promotes the irresponsibility of strategic defaults, they also simultaneously reinforce people's discomfort with the policies that help the homeowners with cash flow problems.

It is interesting that while society expects households to uphold their debt contracts if possible, we don't generally demand the same from businesses. We expect businesses to act in ways that maximize their economic wealth even when those actions seem immoral. There is a double standard between homeowner and business expectations. For example, the Secretary of the Treasury and the U.S. President did not give speeches chastising Morgan Stanley for walking away from five properties in San Francisco in 2009. Those properties had become underwater after losing 50 percent of their value. So, Morgan Stanley defaulted on them and gave them back to the bank.[19] Morgan Stanley decided that defaulting on over a $2 billion deal was in their best interest. Why isn't Morgan Stanley ridiculed as being unethical, obscene, and offensive?

PSYCHOLOGY FURTHER DOWN THE MORTGAGE SUPPLY CHAIN

The consumer is not the only one who suffered from biases in the crisis. Hersh Shefrin claims that the cause of the financial crisis was psychological.[20] Specifically, he details the biases of five participants along the mortgage supply chain. UBS is an investment banking firm that securitized subprime mortgages. But it had fallen behind the performance of its peers. Taking their peers as their reference point caused them to engage in reference-point induced risk seeking behavior. Their overconfidence led them to failure in adequately addressing the risks of their actions. Second, AIG insured these mortgage securities through credit default swaps. They assumed that the historical mortgage default rates would continue to be valid in the future. This is a good example of the representativeness bias. Third, rating agencies like Standard & Poors and Moody's showed groupthink behavior. Groupthink is the psychological predisposition to conform to group expectations. They reached consensus about how to rate the collateralized debt without critically testing and evaluating their assumptions. Even the regulator, the Securities and Exchange Commission, suffered from psychological biases. They ignored the early warning signs of a housing market that was becoming increasingly speculative. This behavior is often described as a confirmation bias, which is a subconscious search to find information that confirms a prior decision and avoids information containing contrary evidence.

Lastly, professor Shefrin analyzes the decisions of the city council of Narvik, a tiny town in Norway. They invested in the complex mortgage securities by borrowing money secured with its power plant's production. The mayor's comments on the matter seem to express their overconfidence in a position they did not completely understand, as shown in the CNBC documentary titled "House of Cards."[21] These investors were overconfident because they felt that the high yields offered were due to other investors' wrong overestimates of default risk. They forgot the most basic theory of finance—expected return and risk are positively related. If return is expected to be high, then the risks are high.

Summary

Psychological biases and decision framing was prevalent in the mortgage crisis. Subprime mortgages were designed to hide high total costs and focus attention on two very salient aspects: low closing costs and low initial monthly payment. Predatory brokers often targeted homeowners undergoing emotional stress, the elderly, and people with low financial literacy because they were more easily manipulated by the decision frames. Once the financial crisis hit, the government provided programs to help the households with severe cash flow problems. Simultaneously, they used behavioral tactics to shame otherwise financially stable households from strategically defaulting on their underwater houses. In general, the social stigma of breaking the social norm on debt contracts inhibited these people from defaulting on underwater homes even though they have economic incentives to do so. Other participants in the mortgage and finance industry also exhibited psychological biases.

Questions

1. Describe how a loan with very high costs to the borrower might appear to have low costs.
2. Is the cross-subsidy of mortgage fees from financially naïve households to financially savvy households good for society? Why?
3. What is the social norm on debt contracts? How and why might that norm be changing through a long recession and weak recovery?
4. Emotional stress truncates the thinking process and negatively influences the decision-making process. What are some examples of emotional stress that a homeowner might experience and how might unscrupulous mortgage brokers identify them?
5. What is groupthink and how might it have impacted the credit ratings of mortgage related securities by credit rating agencies?

Notes

1. This chapter is largely adapted from John Nofsinger, "Household Behavior and Boom/Bust Cycles," *Journal of Financial Stability* 8(2012): 161–173.
2. Robert Shiller, "Understanding Recent Trends in House Prices and Home Ownership," In *Housing, Housing Finance and Monetary Policy, Jackson Hole Conference Series, Federal Reserve Bank of Kansas City*, pp. 85–123, 2008.
3. Irving Janis, *Groupthink*, 2nd ed., Boston: Houghton Mifflin, 1982.
4. John V. Duca, John Muellbauer, and Anthony Murphy, "Housing Markets and the Financial Crisis of 2007–2009: Lessons for the Future," *Journal of Financial Stability* 6(2010): 203–217.
5. Sumit Agarwal, John C. Driscoll, Xavier Gabaix, and David Laibson, "The Age of Reason: Financial Decisions Over the Life Cycle and Implications for Regulation," *Brookings Papers on Economic Activity* 2(2009): 51–117.
6. Victor Stango and Jonathan Zinman, "Exponential Growth Bias and Household Finance," *Journal of Finance* 64(2009): 2807–2849.
7. Oren Bar-Gill, "The Law, Economics, and Psychology of Subprime Mortgage Contracts," *Cornell Law Review* 94(2009): 1073–1151.
8. Yuliya Demyanyk and Otto Van Hemert, "Understanding the subprime mortgage crisis," *Review of Financial Studies* 24(2011): 1848–1880.
9. For the financial decision-making impact of financial literacy, cognitive aging, and emotional stress, see Annamaria Lusardi and Olivia Mitchell, "Baby Boomer Retirement Security: The Role of Planning, Financial Literacy,

and Housing Wealth," *Journal of Monetary Economics* 54(2007): 205–224, George Korniotis and Alok Kumar. "Do Older Investors Make Better Investment Decisions?" *The Review of Economics and Statistics* 93(2011): 244–265, and Mary Frances Luce, James R. Bettman, John W. Payne, *Emotional Decisions: Tradeoff Difficulty and Coping in Consumer Choice*, University of Chicago Press, Chicago, 2001.

10. Lauren E. Willis, "Decision Making and the Limits of Disclosure: The Problem of Predatory Lending: Price," *Maryland Law Review* 65(2006): 707–840.

11. "Prepared Testimony of Ms. Mary Podelco, Hearing on *Predatory Mortgage Lending: The Problem, Impact and Responses*, U.S. Senate Committee on Banking, Housing, and Urban Affairs, July 26, 2001.

12. John Campbell, "Household Finance," *Journal of Finance* 61(2006): 1553–1604.

13. Xavier Gabaix and David Laibson, "Shrouded Attributes, Consumer Myopia, and Information Suppression in Competitive Markets,"*Quarterly Journal of Economics* 121(2006): 505–540.

14. Martin Feldstein, "How to Save an Underwater Mortgage," Wall Street Journal, (August 7, 2009), http://online.wsj.com/article/SB100014 24052970204908604574330883957532854.html.

15. Brent White, "Underwater and not Walking Away: Shame, Fear and the Social Management of the Housing Crisis," *Wake Forest Law Review* 45(2010): 971–1024.

16. Luigi Guiso, Paola Sapienza, and Luigi Zingales, "The Determinants of Attitudes Towards Strategic Default on Mortgages," *Journal of Finance*, forthcoming (2012).

17. Remarks by Secretary Henry M. Paulson, Jr., U.S. Housing and Mortgage Market Update to the National Association of Business Economists (March 3, 2008), http://www.ustreas.gov/press/releases/hp856.htm.

18. President Barack Obama's Foreclosure Speech: Housing Plan, (February 18, 2009), http://www.huffingtonpost.com/2009/02/18/obama-foreclosure-speech_n_167889.html.

19. Shahien Nasiripour, "If Morgan Stanley Walks Away, Why Shouldn't You? Firm Walks Away from 5 Oroperties," *The Huffington Post*, December 17, 2009, http://www.huffingtonpost.com/2009/12/17/if-morgan-stanley-walks-a_n_396543.html.

20. Hersh Shefrin, "How Psychological Pitfalls Generated the Global Financial Crisis," In *Voices of Wisdom: Understanding the Global Financial Crisis of 2007-2009*, L.B. Siegel, editor, Charlottesville, VA: Research Foundation of CFA Institute.

21. See www.cnbc.com/id/28892719.

CREDITS

Page 36: *Source:* "Prospect Theory: An Analysis of Decisions Under Risk," by Daniel Khaneman, Amos Tversky, from *Econometrica*, March 1979, pp. 263–291.

Page 53: "Cognitive Reflection and Decision Making," by Shane Frederick, from *Journal of Economic Perspectives*, 2005. Copyright © 2005 by Journal of Economic Perspectives. Reprinted with permission.

Page 59: *Source:* "Mental Accounting and Consumer Choice," by Richard Thaler, from *Marketing Science*, 1985.

Page 60: "The Red and the Black: Mental Accounting of Savings and Debt," by Drazen Prelec; George Loewenstein, from *Marketing Science*, 17. Copyright © 1998 by Drazen Prelec and George Loewenstein. Reprinted with permission of the Institute for Operations Research and the Management Sciences (INFORMS).

Page 62: *Source:* "Toward a Positive Theory of Consumer Choice," by Richard Thaler, from *Journal of Economics Behavior and Organization*, March 1980.

Page 66: *Source:* "Portfolio Choice and Trading in a Large 401(k) Plan," by Julie Agnew, Pierluigi Balduzzi, and Annika Sundén, from *American Economic Review*, 2003, issue 93.

Page 67: *Source:* "Mental Accounting in Portfolio Choice: Evidence from a Flypaper Effect," by James Choi, David Laibson, and Brigitte Madrian, from *American Economic*, 2009, issue 99.

Page 85: *Source:* "Contrarian Investment, Extrapolation, and Risk," by Josef Lakonishok, Andrei Shleifer, and Robert Vishny, from *Journal of Finance*, 1994, Volume 48. Copyright © 1994 by John Wiley & Sons.

Page 86: *Source:* Investment Company Institute, "Trends in Mutual Fund Investing," various months.

Page 89: *Source:* International Monetary Fund's Coordinated Portfolio Investment Survey for 2005.

Page 91: *Source:* "Participation and Investment Decisions in a Retirement Plan: The Influence of Colleagues' Choices," by Esther Duflo and Emmanuel Saez, from *Journal of Public Economics*, 2002, Volume 85. Copyright © 2002 by Elsevier.

Page 98: *Source:* "Participation and Investment Decisions in a Retirement Plan: The Influence of Colleagues' Choices," by Esther Duflo and Emmanuel Saez, from *Journal of Public Economics*, 2002, Volume 85. Copyright © 2002 by Elsevier.

Page 100: *Source:* "Too Many Cooks Spoil the Profits: Investment Club Performance," by Brad M. Barber and Terrance Odean, *Financial Analysts Journal*, January/February 2000, Volume 56. Copyright © 2000 by the CFA Institute.

Page 102: *Source:* Quote by Mark Twain, October 15, 1888.

INDEX